Metaphors of the Web 2.0

European University Studies

Europäische Hochschulschriften
Publications Universitaires Européennes

Series XIV
Anglo-Saxon Language and Literature

Reihe XIV   Série XIV
Angelsächsische Sprache und Literatur
Langue et littérature anglo-saxonnes

Vol./Bd. 450

PETER LANG
Frankfurt am Main · Berlin · Bern · Bruxelles · New York · Oxford · Wien

Alexander Tokar

Metaphors of the Web 2.0

With Special Emphasis on Social Networks and Folksonomies

PETER LANG
Internationaler Verlag der Wissenschaften

Bibliographic Information published by the Deutsche Nationalbibliothek
The Deutsche Nationalbibliothek lists this publication in the Deutsche Nationalbibliografie; detailed bibliographic data is available in the internet at <http://www.d-nb.de>.

Zugl.: Düsseldorf, Univ., Diss., 2008

Thesis supervision: Prof. Dr. Dieter Stein
Date of oral examination: December 18, 2008

D 61
ISSN 0721-3387
ISBN 978-3-631-58664-8
© Peter Lang GmbH
Internationaler Verlag der Wissenschaften
Frankfurt am Main 2009
All rights reserved.

All parts of this publication are protected by copyright. Any utilisation outside the strict limits of the copyright law, without the permission of the publisher, is forbidden and liable to prosecution. This applies in particular to reproductions, translations, microfilming, and storage and processing in electronic retrieval systems.

www.peterlang.de

Table of Contents

Abbreviations   VIII
Screenshots   X

1. Introduction   1

Part 1 Theoretical issues   5

2. Basic concepts   6
2.1. Metaphor   6
    2.1.1. Definition and structure. Metaphoricity   6
    2.1.2. Grounding   12
    2.1.3. Extension versus intension. Metaphor versus metonymy   14
    2.1.4. Internet master metaphors   16
2.2. Web 2.0   20
    2.2.1. Web 2.0 genres   22
2.3. Web 2.0 metaphors: Preliminaries   23

Part 2 Social networks   27

3. Registration   28
4. Profile   34
4.1. Internet profiles versus traditional profiles   34
4.2. SNS profiles from the referential point of view   40
4.3. Intensional meaning   43
4.4. Origin of the homepage metaphor   46

5. Friend — 52
5.1. Extension — 52
5.2. Intension — 53
    5.2.1. SNS friends versus traditional friends — 53
    5.2.2. Why *friend*? — 57
    5.2.3. Users — 60
5.3. Social networks and traditional concept of friendship — 64

6. Pokes, fives, smiles... — 66
6.1. Creators — 66
    6.1.1. Pokes — 67
    6.1.2. Fives — 68
    6.1.3. SuperFives — 72
    6.1.4. Smiles — 76
6.2. Users — 77
6.3. Summary — 82

Part 3 Folksonomies — 85

7. Tagging — 86
7.1. Tag clouds — 86
    7.1.1. Folksonomies = non-expert taxonomies? — 88
7.2. Search engine metaphor — 92
7.3. Intensional meaning — 94

8. Subscribe — 96
8.1. Extension — 96

	8.1.1. SUBSCRIPTION2.0 versus SUBSCRIPTION1.0	98
8.2.	Linguistic aspects	101
	8.2.1. Why *subscribe*?	101
	8.2.2. The bookmarking metaphor	106
	8.2.3. Intension	107
9.	**Channel**	111
9.1.	Extension	111
9.2.	Television metaphor	112
	9.2.1. YouTube broadcasting. Aspectual analysis	113
	9.2.2. Why *broadcast* and *channel*?	121
	9.2.3. Subscribers	124
9.3.	Intension	127
10.	**Concluding remarks**	130
	References	132

Abbreviations

ABC	American Broadcasting Corporation
ANC	American National Corpus
AOL	America Online
BBC	British Broadcasting Corporation
BNC	British National Corpus
CNN	Cable News Network
CTM	Conceptual Theory of Metaphor
DA	discourse analysis
FAQ	frequently asked question
FTA	face-threatening act
FRIEND1	friend in real-life, i.e., a person whom you know well and regard with affection and trust
FRIEND2	a user of a social-networking Web site who was added as a friend into another user's friends list
HTML	hypertext markup language
ICQ	I seek you/a popular IRC program
IP	Internet protocol
IRC	Internet Relay Chat
KLM	Royal Dutch Airlines
L	lexeme
MIME	Multipurpose Internet Mail Extensions
NSFNET	National Science Foundation Network
NYT	New York Times
PHAC	Public Health Agency of Canada
PM	private message
PT	prototype theory
PROFILE1	traditional profile, i.e., a short biographical sketch/an article about somebody
PROFILE2	member profile of a user of a Web-based service, e.g., Web forum
PROFILE2_1.0	member profile of a user of a Web 1.0 service, e.g., Web forum
PROFILE2_2.0	member profile of a user of a social networking Web site
RSS	Really Simple Syndication/Rich Site Summary/Really Stops Spam
SB	social bookmark/social bookmarking Web site
SIT	situation
SMS	short message service
SNS	social networking Web site

SUBSCRIPTION1.0   subscription to an e-mail newsletter
SUBSCRIPTION2.0   subscription to an RSS feed
SUBSCRIPTIONRW   subscription in real-life (e.g., to a Pay-TV channel)
URL   uniform resource locator
WP   Washington Post
XML   extensible markup language
Ψ   obligatory participant of a situation

x

Screenshots

Screenshot 1. Fake profiles on Facebook	31
Screenshot 2. NYT profile of Hillary Clinton	35
Screenshot 3. Blackcat's profile on ICQ (www.icq.com)	35-36
Screenshot 4. Hillary Clinton's description on her MySpace profile	42
Screenshot 5. Friends on hi5.com	42
Screenshot 6. "Friend Subscriptions" section on MySpace	63
Screenshot 7. "Friend Updates" section on hi5	63
Screenshot 8. Fives on hi5	69
Screenshot 9. The "Stats" section on a hi5 profile	70
Screenshot 10. SuperFives on hi5	73
Screenshot 11. A smile on Friendster	77
Screenshot 12. SuperPokes on Facebook	81
Screenshot 13. Tag cloud on Flickr	86
Screenshot 14. Site Map of www.whitehouse.gov	87
Screenshot 15. A photo of a KLM airplane on Flickr	90
Screenshot 16. Education-feed on www.washingtonpost.com	96
Screenshot 17. Feeds on Internet Explorer	97
Screenshot 18. Feed options on Internet Explorer	97
Screenshot 19. "Bookmarks" on Mozilla Firefox	106
Screenshot 20. YouTube symbol	112
Screenshot 21. Broadcast options on YouTube	113
Screenshot 22. Gaijin Navi videos	118
Screenshot 23. "Subscribers" section on a YouTube channel	125
Screenshot 24. Subscribing to Britney Spears' YouTube channel	126

1. Introduction

> The Internet is not something that you just dump something on. It's not a big truck. It's a **series of tubes**. (Senator Ted Stevens during the Senate hearings on network neutrality, 28.06.2006)
>
> Generally speaking, I don't look for information in a rubbish heap. And the Internet is a **rubbish heap**. (Mikhail Leontyev in an interview to Echo of Moscow, 23.07.2008, my translation)

It is a well-known fact that our most important abstract concepts (e.g., emotions) are usually characterized by metaphorical pluralism (Lakoff and Johnson 1999: 70), i.e., conceptualization of a single target concept in terms of multiple source concepts. For example, LOVE is simultaneously A UNITY OF TWO COMPLEMENTARY PARTS (e.g., *she's my better half*), A FLUID IN A CONTAINER (e.g., *she was overflowing with love*), A PHYSICAL FORCE (e.g., *I was magnetically drawn to her*), CLOSENESS (e.g., *they're very close*), POSSESSION (e.g., *you're mine and I'm yours*), INSANITY (e.g., *I'm crazy about you*), WAR (e.g., *she conquered him*), MAGIC (e.g., *she is bewitching*), FIRE (e.g., *I'm burning with love*), etc. (Kövecses 2000: 26-27).

In addition to abstract concepts, metaphorical pluralism often emerges when, as a consequence of a technological innovation, language users need to verbalize (i.e., find expressions that can be used to refer to) a new, highly complex concrete concept such as, for example, the Internet (Gehring 2004: 10). Indeed, given the complexity and the multi-functionality of the global computer network—as is well-known, the Internet is used in a variety of ways, e.g., for communication, commerce, entertainment, etc.—it is not surprising that in addition to being a *series of tubes* and a *rubbish heap*, the Internet is also often referred to as *agora, electronic frontier, cyberspace, global village, empyrean realm, information superhighway, ocean of information, container, prosthesis for the senses or limbs, city*, etc.

Each of these metaphors seems to constitute what Gozzi (1994a: 321) calls *master metaphor*, i.e., a metaphor "organi[zing] a group of mini-metaphors into a coherent cluster" and thereby attempting to explain the nature of the Internet (or any other complex phenomenon) by highlighting a particular aspect of its use (or a particularly salient feature associated with the phenomenon under consideration). For example, the cyberspace metaphor emphasizes the novelty and the exceptionality of the Internet, e.g., that cyberspace should be immune from regulation through traditional territorial governments because it does not lie within their borders (Blavin and Cohen 2002: 275). In the empyrean realm metaphor, the focus is on a utopian conception of the Internet as the technological implementation of Christian Heaven (Mihalache 2002: 294). The information superhighway metaphor highlights the transportation of information as the main function of the Internet (Blavin and Cohen 2002: 270), whereas in the container metaphor the Web is represented as a container (e.g., a library or an archive) where information is stored (Markham 2003; cf. Porto Requejo 2007: 197-198). And so on.

Besides master metaphors (many of which can be seen as philosophical conceptions of what the Internet is), there exist a number of metaphorical expressions which, unlike master metaphors, do not apply to the Internet in its entirety but only to a particular Internet-related concept. For example, movement on the Web (e.g., *surf/cruse/navigate the Web*, *browse Web pages*, *visit a Web site*, etc.), structure of cyberspace (e.g., *Web site*, *Web page*, *Web portal*, etc.), particular Internet application/software (e.g., *electronic mail*, *virtual world*, *virtual store*, *electronic journal*, *search engine*, *firewall*, etc.), etc. As Meyer et al. (1997) point out, Internet terminology abounds in metaphorical expressions because they,

> by allowing computer users to see a potentially complex concept in terms of a well-known and simple one, aid users in understanding and remembering new concepts. At the same time, metaphorical terms allow users to associate unfamiliar concepts with old, "comfortable" ones, thereby helping to palliate technostress. Software developers have become keenly aware of the "user friendliness" of metaphors, as illustrated by the numerous metaphorical terms found in the vocabulary of user interfaces [...] (pp. 3-4; for a detailed discussion of the role of metaphor in designing software interfaces, see Wozny 1989, Madsen 1994, Smilowitz 1996)

Given these facts, it is not surprising that Internet metaphors have already been extensively dealt with in numerous studies. For example, Gozzi (1994a, 1994b, 1997, 2006), Helmers et al. (1994), Hofmann (1996), Palmquist (1996), Stefik (1996), Canzler et al. (1997), Meyer et al. (1997), Rohrer (1997, 2001), Baumgärtel (1998), Reichertz (1998), Barbatsis et al. (1999), Maglio and Matlock (1999), Ratzan (2000), Woiskunski (2001), Blavin and Cohen (2002), Jamet (2002), Jansen (2002, 2005), Lemley (2002), Mihalache (2002), Schnadwinkel (2002), Tomaszewski (2002), Markham (2003), Núñez (2004), Gehring (2004), Lombard (2005), Cohen (2007), Porto Requejo (2007), Tokar (2007).

However, none of these studies (including the most recent ones) deal with what during the last three years came to be known as *Web 2.0* (O'Reilly 2005), i.e., a cover term for a variety of services such as social networking sites (SNSs) (e.g., MySpace, Facebook, hi5, etc.), social bookmarks (SBs) (e.g., Delicious, StumbleUpon, Furl, etc.), video- and photo-sharing services like YouTube and Flickr, blogging sites like LiveJournal and Blogger, wikis like Wikipedia and Wikibooks, etc.—Web sites which, in contrast to traditional 1.0 Web sites (i.e., classical personal Web sites, Web sites of traditional print and electronic media, commercial Web sites, etc.) mainly contain user-generated content. For example, profile pages maintained by members of an SNS, URLs of favorite Web pages bookmarked by users of an SB, videos and photos uploaded on services like YouTube and Flickr, a blog entry posted to LiveJournal, an article published on Wikipedia, etc.

The present study is thus an attempt to fill the research gap by analyzing some of the metaphorical expressions associated with two particular Web 2.0 practices: SNSs and folksonomies. The latter term stands for a number of Web 2.0 services of various genres (e.g., social bookmarks, video- and photo-sharing services, blogging sites, etc.) whose distinctive feature is collaborative tagging, i.e., the practice whereby users of these services assign freely chosen keywords to the content which they would like to make findable for other users (Mika 2005: 523).

This study will deal with seven metaphorical expressions—*sign up*, *profile*, *friend*, *poke*, *tag*, *subscribe*, and *channel*—which can often be found in the context of SNS and folksonomic Web sites and can therefore be considered Web 2.0 metaphors. (Moreover, as we will see, many of these expressions—or, being more exact, things which they denote—can be considered the defining characteristics of social networks and folksonomies.) The primary objective is to analyze both the referential and the conceptual aspects of these terms' semantics, i.e., what these words stand for and which concepts they signify in the Web 2.0 era.

The study has the following structure. Chapter 2 *Basic concepts* introduces the main tenets of the Conceptual Theory of Metaphor (Lakoff and Johnson 1980, 1999). The reason for this is not only that this theory, to a very large extent, underlies my own understanding of metaphor. Much more important is that unlike other metaphor theories, the approach of Lakoff and Johnson provides a theoretical framework for analyzing systematic metaphors, i.e., metaphors characterized by systematic correspondences between their source and target domains. (And as will be shown in chapters 3-9, each of the metaphors chosen for this study is a metaphor of this type.) In addition to this and some other purely linguistic issues (e.g., differences between extensional and intensional approaches to meaning, factors determining the degree of metaphoricity of a metaphorical expression, the notion of a semi-phraseme, etc.), the chapter will touch on some specific issues relevant for the discussion of Internet metaphors. For example, what is exactly a master metaphor? And do terms like *information superhighway*, *cyberspace*, *electronic frontier*, *series of tubes*, and other Internet master metaphors have anything in common? Finally, the chapter will elaborate on the term *Web 2.0*: What are the main differences between Web 2.0 and Web 1.0 and are these differences reflected in new metaphors applying to the former but not to the latter? The main part of the study are, however, chapters 3-9. Each of these chapters represents an independent case study containing the semantic analysis of an individual metaphorical expression named above.

PART I THEORETICAL ISSUES

2. Basic concepts

Since the focus of this study is on metaphors of the Web 2.0, it seems reasonable to start with the terms *metaphor* and *Web 2.0*.

2.1. Metaphor

2.1.1. Definition and structure. Metaphoricity.

In the Conceptual Theory of Metaphor (CTM) (see Lakoff and Johnson 1980, 1999; cf. Kövecses 2002, 2005, 2006), metaphor is defined as a systematic correspondence between two different domains of experience one of which (the target domain) is partially understood in terms of the other (the source domain), so that the former can be said to be the latter. For example, ELECTRONIC JOURNAL IS A TRADITIONAL PRINT JOURNAL (i.e., TRADITIONAL PRINT JOURNAL is the source domain for the target domain ELECTRONIC JOURNAL), ELECTRONIC MAIL IS TRADITIONAL MAIL, THE INTERNET IS A HIGHWAY, etc. (A conceptual domain is "a more generalized 'background' knowledge configuration against which conceptualization is achieved" (Taylor 2002: 195). For example, we need the concept of electronic mail system in order to understand what an e-mail message is. Accordingly, the former is the domain against which the latter is conceptualized.)

One of the main CTM hallmarks is that it distinguishes between conceptual metaphors and metaphorical expressions. The former are structures like the just named E-JOURNAL IS A PRINT JOURNAL, E-MAIL IS TRADITIONAL MAIL, THE INTERNET IS A HIGHWAY, etc., which are believed to be

> ensembles of neurons in different parts of the brain connected by neural circuitry. The ensembles of neurons located in different parts of the brain are the source and target domains, and the physical neural circuitry that connects them is the mappings. (Kövecses 2006: 120; cf. Johnson 2007: ch. 8, Lakoff 2008)

Metaphorical expressions are, by contrast, words that are used to express aspects of a given conceptual metaphor (Lakoff 1987: 384) or, as Deignan (2005: 14) puts it, *realize* it linguistically. For example, expressions pertaining to the source domain AUTOMOBILE HIGHWAY that can be used to refer to the target domain INTERNET (e.g., *lane* in *Cable and telephone companies are talking, however, about creating a two-tiered Internet with a fast lane and a slow lane* (New York Times = NYT, 03.01.2007), *speed bump* in *They say there is a value to an occasional speed bump on the information superhighway* (NYT, 15.08.2004), *drive* in *If you are too young to drive on a regular superhighway, then you're probably too young to drive unsupervised on the information superhighway* (NYT,

06.07.2004), etc.) can be considered linguistic realizations of the conceptual metaphor THE INTERNET IS AN AUTOMOBILE HIGHWAY.

In stark contrast to other metaphor theories (for a good overview, see Rolf 2005), the focus of CTM is not on the mere documentation of metaphorical expressions like *drive on the information superhighway* but on the identification of the structure of a conceptual metaphor represented by ontological and epistemic mappings of the source onto the target. (Metaphorical expressions are, however, regarded as the main empirical evidence for the existence of a particular mapping.) Ontological mappings are mappings of entities from the source domain onto the corresponding entities in the target domain (Lakoff 1987: 387). For example, in the electronic journal metaphor, (1) authors, readers, editors-in-chief, members of the editorial board, etc., of traditional print journals map onto authors, readers, editors-in-chief, members of the editorial board, etc., of e-journals; (2) articles, reviews, discussion papers, etc., published in traditional journals onto articles, reviews, discussion papers, etc., published in e-journals; (3) peer-reviewing of traditional journals onto peer-reviewing of e-journals; (4) publishers of traditional journals onto people/organizations running e-journals' Web sites; (5) paper on which traditional journals are published onto e-journals' Web sites; etc.

As for epistemic mappings, they are defined as "correspondences between knowledge about the source domain and corresponding knowledge about the target domain" (ibid. p. 387). For example, the quality of an article published in a traditional print journal is usually warranted by peer-reviewing—the procedure whereby all submitted articles are subjected to the scrutiny of reviewers, i.e., people who are experts in the same field as the author of a submitted article. The same can be said about (at least some) electronic journals. For example, *Language@Internet* is "an open-access, *peer-reviewed*, scholarly electronic journal" (www.languageatinternet.de). That the entity "peer-reviewing" equally applies to both the source domain TRADITIONAL PRINT JOURNAL and the target domain ELECTRONIC JOURNAL is because of the mapping of the corresponding knowledge about the former—i.e., that an academic article cannot be published without being subjected to the scrutiny of reviewers—onto the latter.

Closely related to epistemic mappings are entailments (Kövecses 2006: 123). An entailment is anything you can infer about the target domain, given your knowledge of the source domain. For example, as argued by Blavin and Cohen (2002: 269), the information superhighway metaphor—a popular metaphorical conception of the Internet of the early 1990s—entails (1) suitability for state involvement; (2) ephemerality of information; and (3) low degree of exceptionalism.

The inference that the Internet is suitable for state involvement arises because automobile highways are usually built and regulated by the state. Indeed, "if the Internet is a highway, then the government can regulate it for the safety of those who pass on it" (pp. 169-170). Among other things, this seems to suggest that people are not a priori entitled to have access to the Internet. That is, before being permitted to "drive" on the information superhighway, an Internet user will have to obtain a document similar to a driver's license in the automobile world.

Ephemerality of information refers to the idea that the Internet is not a container where information "resides," but a conduit where it is transferred. Like *suitability for state involvement, ephemerality of information* can be seen as an entailment of the source concept AUTOMOBILE HIGHWAY, for, as Blavin and Cohen point out,

> though cars use the highway to travel the distance between two destinations, no one "lives" or "resides" on the highway; in fact, one of the first rules of driving is never to stop your car while on the road. (p. 270)

Finally, *low degree of exceptionalism* means that there is nothing special in the way the Internet transports information:

> Software can be transported to a computer user through the interstate telephone lines of the world wide web, just as it can travel the interstate highways in the back of a truck to a computer store and the eventual end user. In this manner, the Internet and more traditional means of transportation, such as highways, serve the same purpose of moving goods across state lines. (p. 271)

Accordingly, rules governing the use of highways as well as those of traditional means of communication should also be appropriate for the Internet.

At the same time, however, it is important to note that all conceptual metaphors are characterized by partial metaphorical structuring (Lakoff and Johnson 1980: 52; cf. Lakoff and Wehling 2008: 28), i.e., only some entities and only some knowledge about the source domain can apply to the target domain. For example, despite the entailment that an Internet user must possess a "driver's license" in order to be permitted to "drive" on the information superhighway, there is no "driver's license" for the Internet: No one has to take a "driver's exam" in order to be able to use the global computer network. Likewise, in contrast to traditional mail, electronic mail lacks the concept of an envelope as well as of a stamp. That is, e-mail users do not have to insert e-mails into digital envelopes. And they do not have to buy digital stamps in order to be able to send their messages to other users (Stefik 1996: 115-120).

Finally, it must be pointed out that the degree of systematicity of ontological mappings seems to be one of the major factors determining the metaphoricity of a metaphorical expression: The more entities of the source domain have correspondences in the target domain, the less metaphorical is the metaphor in question. For example, almost everything we know about traditional journals (in terms of entities) is also characteristic of e-journals: Both the former and the latter have editors-in chief, members of the editorial board, reviewers as well people who write and read articles that are published there. Both the former and the latter publish articles, reviews, discussion papers, and the material alike. Even the main epistemic difference—the fact that traditional journals are print journals, whereas e-journals are published online—is, from the CTM point of view, a similarity between the source domain TRADITIONAL JOURNAL and the target domain ELECTRONIC JOURNAL since it constitutes an ontological correspondence between the former and the latter, i.e., the element "paper" in the source domain TRADITIONAL JOURNAL can be said to map onto the element "e-journal's Web site" in the target domain ELECTRONIC JOURNAL. The consequence of this is that the term *e-journal* is hardly metaphorical. Thus, as can be inferred from the definition below, *e-journal* means "e-journal," i.e., a journal that is published on the Internet:

Electronic Journal
A journal which is available via the Internet. The journal is usually, but not always, also available in paper format.
http://lis.tees.ac.uk/glossary/defgh.cfm?&TS=1

In contrast, the term *firewall* does not mean "firewall" but a "computer program or hardware that blocks unauthorized access":

Firewall
A firewall is a piece of hardware or software program which protects a computer or network from attacks from intruders and hackers.
http://www.cliftonpark.org/articles/content.asp?MemberID=3798

Firewall
Hardware and/or software used to prevent computer hackers from getting into a computer system.
http://www.ukorbit.com/computer-glossary.htm

That *firewall* does not mean "firewall," whereas *e-journal* means "journal" is because the latter is a very systematic metaphor in which many entities of the source domain TRADITIONAL JOURNAL map onto the corresponding entities in the target domain ELECTRONIC JOURNAL. *Firewall* is, quite to the contrary, a very unsystematic metaphor which, among other things, lacks the concept of fire. That is, HACKING IS **NOT** FIRE-RAISING, as the term *firewall* may seem to entail, but BURGLARY (Tokar 2007: 214). A hacker does not intend to destroy another user's computer by setting it on fire. Instead, he is a burglar who breaks into a computer system trying to steal information. Given that "fire" is one of the defining characteristics of real-world firewalls (i.e., fire-resistant walls designed to prevent the spread of fire), it is not surprising that its non-mapping onto the target domain COMPUTER FIREWALLS makes the term *firewall* an easily recognizable metaphor.

In addition to systematicity of ontological mappings, the degree of metaphoricity also depends on whether a metaphorical expression fulfills the additional naming requirement (Dobrovol'skij and Piirainen 2005: 18), i.e., is perceived as an additional way of verbalizing the concept which it denotes. The point here is that metaphors (or, more generally, expressions that underwent semantic reinterpretation) fulfilling the additional naming requirement tend to have a higher degree of metaphoricity than those which do not. Thus, even though the majority of English speakers no longer know why the idiom *kick the bucket* means "die," all of them know that *kick the bucket* does not mean what it literally stands for (Nunberg et al. 1994: 492). The same, however, cannot be said about the idiom *play a role*: No one seems to be aware that the literal meaning of *play a role* is not "be important" as in, e.g., *schools play an important role in society*, but "play a role in a theatre" (Dobrovol'skij 1997: 39). The reason for this is that in contrast to *kick the bucket* which is not the primary way of verbalizing the concept of dying—the primary expression is *die*—*play a role* has become a primary expression for the concept of being important and has therefore completely lost its original idiomaticity.

Likewise, the information superhighway metaphor seems to have a higher degree of metaphoricity than the firewall metaphor, even though the former is undoubtedly much more systematic than the latter with regard to its ontological structure. (That is, for example, in the information superhighway metaphor, (1) driving in the source domain AUTOMOBILE HIGHWAY maps onto using the global computer network in the target domain INTERNET; (2) cars onto computers; (3) car drivers onto Internet users; (4) speed of a car onto speed of an Internet connection; (5) distance you drove on a car onto your Internet traffic; (6) traffic jams, road bumps, road signs, etc., onto all kinds of problems we have to deal with when using the global computer network; etc.) The impression that *information superhighway* is more metaphorical than *firewall* arises because the former is an instance of a domain construction (Sullivan 2007: 6), i.e., a metaphorical phrase like *spiritual wealth* in which the target domain SPIRITUAL ACCOMPLISHMENTS is evoked by the modifying adjective *spiritual* and the source domain MATERIAL ACQUISITIONS by the head noun *wealth*. In a similar way, in *information superhighway*, the target domain INTERNET is evoked by the modifier *information* and the source domain AUTOMOBILE HIGHWAY by the head noun *highway*. Summarizing: In both *spiritual wealth* and *information superhighway*, the metaphorical meanings depend on the modifiers *spiritual* and *information*. If these are removed, both *wealth* and *highway* will be interpreted literally, i.e., the first thing that will come to mind upon hearing *wealth* and *highway* without *spiritual* and *information* will most likely be material wealth and an automobile highway, not spiritual wealth and the Internet. As for *fire-*

wall, it is clear that this term does not need an additional target domain expression like, e.g., *computer* in order to evoke the target domain meaning "computer firewall." *Firewall* can do this on its own. For example, the sentence *I have a good firewall* can be easily understood as "I have a good computer firewall" without the modifier *computer*. According to Deignan (2005: 39-47), this is an important evidence for the loss of the original metaphoricity: If a metaphorical expression does not depend on additional target domain expressions for the evocation of its target domain meaning, then the metaphorical meaning is no longer perceived as an extension of the expression's original meaning (e.g., "automobile highway" > "Internet"), but as either a polyseme (e.g., *firewall*: 1) a fire-resistant wall designed to prevent the spread of fire; 2) a computer program that prevents hackers from breaking into a computer system) or even a homonym of the original source concept (e.g., *cookie* as a sweet biscuit and *cookie* as a small text file that certain Web sites attach to a user's hard drive while s/he is browsing them).

But why is this so? Why is *firewall* less metaphorical than *information superhighway*? As suggested above, the answer to this question is the fulfillment of the additional naming requirement by *information superhighway* and the non-fulfillment of this requirement by *firewall*. Indeed, *information superhighway* is not the primary way of verbalizing the concept INTERNET: the primary expression for the concept of the global computer network is *Internet* (or *Web*, or *global computer network*), not *highway*, *agora*, *frontier*, *empyrean realm*, *series of tubes*, etc. In contrast, *firewall* has always been the primary expression for the concept of a computer firewall and has therefore, like *play a role*, almost completely lost its original metaphoricity. That is, since *firewall* has always been the primary way of referring to a computer firewall, the meaning "computer firewall" is now perceived as one of the primary meanings of the expression *firewall*. As a result, language users no longer need the concept of a fire-resistant wall in order to understand what a computer firewall is. (In our mental lexicon, there exists a separate entry for both kinds of firewalls.) The consequence of this is the gradual loss of the original metaphoricity.

In the case of *information superhighway* which fulfills the additional naming requirement, the situation is reverse. The original metaphoricity did not disappear because *information superhighway* has always been an additional expression for the concept of the global computer network so that the meaning "Internet" has always been perceived as a non-primary meaning of *highway*. That is, speakers of English have always been aware that THE INTERNET IS **NOT** AN AUTOMOBILE HIGHWAY but is only in some respects similar to it. Accordingly, if the Internet is not a highway but is nevertheless called a *highway*, then the original metaphoricity has to be retained since it explains why *highway* can be used as a synonym of the Internet.

2.1.2. Grounding

Another important issue is the question of how conceptual metaphors like E-JOURNAL IS A PRINT JOURNAL, E-MAIL IS TRADITIONAL MAIL, THE INTERNET IS A HIGHWAY, etc., come into existence. As suggested by Lakoff and Johnson (1980), the answer to this question is either experiential co-occurrence or experiential similarity between the source and target domain:

> An example of experiential co-occurrence would be the MORE IS UP metaphor [e.g., *skyrocketing prices*]. MORE IS UP is grounded in the co-occurrence of two types of experience: adding more of a substance and seeing the level of the substance rise. [...] An example of experiential similarity is LIFE IS A GAMBLING GAME metaphor [e.g., *he's holding all the aces*], where one experiences actions in life as gambles, and the possible consequences of those actions are perceived as winning and losing. (p. 155)

In addition to experiential co-occurrence and experiential similarity, conceptual metaphors can also be grounded in a phonetic similarity between source and target domain expressions. Consider, for example, the conceptual metaphor SOFTWARE IS GARMENT (Tokar 2007: 218) which in Russian is linguistically realized by the software-related use of (1) *šarovary* (literally, "wide trousers") meaning "shareware" (i.e., a computer program that is distributed on the try-before-you-buy basis); (2) *samonadevajušiesja šarovary* (literally, "self-dressing trousers") denoting a self-extracting archive of a shareware; and (3) *primerjat'* (literally, "to put on a garment in order to see whether it fits and looks nice") to refer to testing a shareware. That SOFTWARE was in Russian metaphorized as GARMENT is only because the original English expression *shareware* is phonetically similar to the Russian word *šarovary*, not because of either experiential co-occurrence or experiential similarity between the source domain GARMENT and the target domain SOFTWARE.

Or consider the information superhighway metaphor. Analyzed synchronically, this metaphor can be said to be grounded in a functional (or, using Lakoff and Johnson's terminology, *experiential*) similarity between the source domain AUTOMOBILE HIGHWAY and the target domain INTERNET: Both are means of transport (Markham 2003). However, from a diachronic perspective, the grounding of this metaphor is the fact that the former U.S. Vice President Albert Gore, Jr.—who is often credited with being the inventor (or at least the main popularizer) of the term *information superhighway*—

> is the son of Albert Gore, Snr., who served as Senator from Tennessee from 1959 through 1971 and was a force behind the Federal Aid to Highways Acts. These acts substantially increased federal funding in the national system of interstate and defense highways. Creating highways is in the Gore family tradition. (Stefik 1996: xvii)

Taking this into account, it can be conjectured that had it not been this fact, the term *information superhighway* would perhaps never be coined (Gehring 2004: 95).

Finally, it must be noted that conceptual metaphors are often grounded in themselves. Thus it is clear that electronic mail would never come into existence if the creators of e-mail systems had not mapped some of their knowledge about traditional mail onto the concept of the global computer network—e.g., that the latter can also be used for asynchronous communication—and in this way decided to create e-mail. Likewise, e-journals would never be launched if scholars had not mapped some of their knowledge about traditional print journals onto the target domain INTERNET—e.g., that if all submissions are subject to peer-reviewing warranting the quality of what is published online, then there is no difference whether an article is published on paper or on an e-journal's Web site—and in this way decided to launch e-journals. Summarizing: In the world of technology, conceptual metaphor (characterized by the conscious non-mapping of some elements and some knowledge about the source onto the target) is very often the motivation triggering a particular innovation. As an illustration of this, consider the below description of the e-journal *Language@Internet*:

> As an electronic journal, *Language@Internet* departs from traditional print journals in at least three respects:
> Online access: *Language@Internet* is only available online, through a freely accessible online content system. [...]
> Speedy review and publication: To ensure timely publication of current research, *Language@Internet* aims at sending decisions to authors within three months from the time of submission and publishing accepted manuscripts within a period of no more than four months.
> Innovative formats: The online platform allows for new and innovative publication formats, as for example the publication of research materials and comprehensive data sets in digital format, including audio-visual material, online presentations, and electronic databases.
> http://www.languageatinternet.de/about.journal_html

Reading this description, it becomes clear that the reason why "online access," "speedy review and publication," and "innovative formats" are characteristic of *Language@Internet* is the deliberate and conscious non-mapping of some of the *Language@Internet* founders' knowledge about traditional print journals onto ELECTRONIC JOURNALS, i.e., being unsatisfied with certain characteristics of print journals, *Language@Internet* founders decided to launch an e-journal departing from traditional journals in such respects as open access, speedy publication, and innovative formats. In a similar way, it can be suggested that electronic mail was invented because of its creators' wish to get rid of envelopes and stamps (as well as of some other entities associated with traditional mail) in order to considerably simplify and expedite asynchronous communication.

2.1.3. Extension versus intension. Metaphor versus metonymy.

Concluding the purely theoretical part of this chapter, a few words must be said about the differences between extensional and intensional approaches to meaning. The former attempts to establish a correlation between words and aspects of the world (e.g., things, states, happenings, etc.) which words can refer to, e.g., between the word *cat* and a particular cat referred to in the sentence *I love my cat* (Cruse 2004: 26). The intensional approach, by contrast, is concerned with what can be called *conceptual meaning*, i.e., concept (or mental description) associated with a particular linguistic expression, e.g., the concept of a cat represented by a set of distinctive features (e.g., [+meowing]) distinguishing cats from other animals (ibid. p. 27).

That extension and intension are indeed two different aspects of meaning can be illustrated by the famous example *the Prime-Minister of Great Britain* vs. *the Leader of the Labor Party* (Kortmann 2005: 197). Analyzed extensionally, these two phrases can be said to have the same referential meaning: Mr. Gordon Brown who is currently the Prime-Minister of Great Britain and the Leader of the Labor Party. However, from the intensional point of view, these expressions are not synonymous: *the Prime-Minister of Great Britain* signifies a different concept than *the Leader of the Labor Party*.

For another example, consider the term *electronic journal*. In the previous sections it was taken for granted that *e-journal* is a metaphorical expression which linguistically realizes the conceptual metaphor ELECTRONIC JOURNAL IS A TRADITIONAL PRINT JOURNAL. However, given the differences between the two approaches to meaning, it is clear that this claim can only be based on the extensional approach, i.e., *e-journal* can be considered a referential metaphor because it refers to a thing different from a traditional print journal. But what about the term's intensional meaning? As stated earlier, *e-journal* seems to have a fully compositional meaning "journal published on the Internet." In other words, the constituent *journal* signifies the same concept "journal" when used to refer to an electronic journal and a traditional print journal. Accordingly, *e-journal* is not a metaphor.

Finally, consider the term *digital library*, another popular metaphorical conception of the Internet of the early 1990s:

> Since the mid-1980's with the advent of NSFNET [National Science Foundation Network] the volume of traffic, the number of interconnected networks and the functionality of the networks has grown and continues to grow exponentially. The entire assemblage of linked networks using the IP communications protocol throughout the world is now referred to as the Internet. It is a network of networks, which within the U.S., links one third of all two year and four year colleges and universities, many primary and secondary schools, public and private institutions, commercial enterprises, individuals in their homes, and foreign in-

stitutions in sixty countries. Information sources accessed via the Internet are the ingredients of a **digital library**.
http://www.nsf.gov/pubs/stis1993/nsf93141/nsf93141.txt

In this excerpt from the 1994 Digital Library Initiative, the term *digital library* stands for the totality of the Internet, i.e., all information sources that can be accessed by means of the global computer network. Like *electronic journal*, *digital library* can be considered a referential metaphor because it refers to a thing different from a traditional library. However, from the intensional point of view, *digital library* seems to involve a metonymic extension of the concept of a traditional library: "collection of selected information" > "collection of all kinds of information." Thus, as defined by WordNet, a traditional library is "a collection of literary documents or records kept for reference or borrowing" or "a building that houses a collection of books and other materials for reading and study." In stark contrast to this, the Internet is often described as a collection of non-selected information. For example, Jampolski (1998: 241) points out that the Internet contains many things which can never be found in traditional libraries and archives, e.g., pornography, commercial information, etc. (Recall that, according to Mikhail Leontyev, THE INTERNET IS A RUBBISH HEAP.)

To prove that *library* in *digital library* is a metonym of *library* in, e.g., *Library of Congress*, let us consider in which respects metonymy is different from metaphor. In traditional diachronic semantics, metonymy is defined as semantic change based on contiguity of senses—i.e., there exists a real link between the original and the novel meaning—whereas metaphor is said to involve a perceived similarity between the former and the latter (Hock 1986: 285). In cognitive linguistics, the contrast between the two processes is usually described as *cross-domain mapping* (metaphor) versus *within-domain mapping* (metonymy). According to Lakoff and Turner (1989),

— In *metaphor*, there are two conceptual domains, and one is understood in terms of the other.
— In *metaphor*, a whole schematic structure (with two or more entities) is mapped onto another schematic structure [...]
None of this is true in metonymy.
— Metonymy involves only one conceptual domain. A metonymic mapping occurs within a single domain, not across domains [...]
— In *metonymy*, one entity in a schema is taken as standing for one other entity in the same schema, or the schema as a whole. (p. 103)

As for *digital library*, it is clear that here we are dealing with a within-domain mapping, namely, the mapping of "collection of selected information" onto "collection of all kinds of information" within the COLLECTION domain. Or, alternatively, we can argue that there exists a real link between the meanings "collection of selected information" and "collection of all kinds of information": both meanings have the semantic component "collection."

To conclude, many Internet metaphors are referential, not intensional metaphors. This is a very important finding which, as we will see in Chapters 3-9, is also true of many Web 2.0 metaphors which, similar to *electronic journal* and *digital library*, can be considered metaphors only from the extensional but not from the intensional point of view.

2.1.4. Internet master metaphors

Finally, before turning the attention to Web 2.0, let us have a brief look at Internet master metaphors, i.e., terms like *information superhighway*, *digital library*, *empyrean realm*, *electronic frontier*, *agora*, *cyberspace*, etc. The most interesting question here is why the global computer network was/is being analogized to these particular source domains. Do they have anything in common?

To answer this question, it is, first of all, necessary to give a more precise definition of the term *master metaphor*. As argued by Gozzi (1994a), a master metaphor

> organizes a group of mini-metaphors into a coherent cluster. Thus we could talk about different technologies as *on ramps* to the *information highway*. One television executive, concerned about possible negative effects on broadcasting stations, warned that there will be *drive-by shootings* on the *information superhighway*. Other companies worried about becoming *road kill*, as the new electronic networks could put many existing enterprises out of business. (pp. 321-322)

Given this description, it appears that for Gozzi a master metaphor is simply an expression representing a conceptual domain (i.e., a concept of a more inclusive nature against which conceptualization is achieved). For example, HIGHWAY is the domain for such concepts as driving, cars, speed bumps, lanes, road signs, traffic jams, etc. In CTM, however, the term *master metaphor* is reserved for (very!) abstract conceptual structures which, unlike *information superhighway*, *digital library*, *empyrean realm*, *electronic frontier*, *agora*, *cyberspace*, etc., are usually not visible in language. Consider, for example, the EVENT-STRUCTURE metaphor in which states are conceptualized as regions bounded in space and changes in states as movements between such regions (Lakoff and Johnson 1999: 180, 183). Linguistically, this metaphor is realized by the use of spatial prepositions and motion verbs to denote interactions with abstract states, e.g., *being in love, moving towards democracy, coming out of depression, entering the state of euphoria*, etc. That is, when somebody is in love, s/he is physically inside of the region "love." When a country is moving towards democracy, it is going from the region "non-democracy" to the region "democracy." And so on.

Particularly interesting about the EVENT-STRUCTURE metaphor is that language users seem to be unaware of its existence. Thus a laymen will most likely have difficulties in figuring out how love can be a region bounded in space if it is a feeling, and how moving towards democracy can involve changing a country's spatial location if no such thing is actually taking place (i.e., a country *moving* towards democracy is not moving anywhere). The same, however, is not true of *information superhighway*, *digital library*, *empyrean realm*, *electronic frontier*, *agora*, *cyberspace*, etc., which, as shown earlier, are often used as synonyms of the global computer network and therefore cannot qualify as master metaphors from the CTM point of view.

Given this fact, let us attempt to find the Internet true (or super) master metaphors, i.e., abstract structures which, like the EVENT-STRUCTURE metaphor, are not visible in language but nevertheless structure our entire conceptualization of the concept of the global computer network.

As proposed by Markham (2003), the two Internet super master metaphors are the metaphors THE INTERNET IS A TOOL and THE INTERNET IS A PLACE. The former can be divided into three sub-metaphors: THE INTERNET IS A CONDUIT, THE INTERNET IS A CONTAINER, and THE INTERNET IS A PROSTHESIS FOR THE SENSES OR LIMBS.

As for the conduit metaphor, the Internet is indeed a conduit because, like other conduits, it serves as a means of transport:

> Conduits are means of transport from one place to another place. Whether we call the Internet a conduit directly is less important than the fact that our linguistic frame expresses those characteristics that are perceived as central to the technology. Pipes, straws, or electricity; the form is not as important as the emphasis. Conduit, as a metaphor, focuses on the Internet as a medium for transmission of information from one location to another. (Markham 2003: online)

Markham is right in her implicit suggestion that the Internet is not often directly referred to as a conduit. (The search for "Internet is a conduit" using Google which I conducted on September 06, 2008 produced only 836 results.) But it is often called a *highway* (in the context of *information superhighway*) which is a hyponym of *conduit*: That is, a highway is a kind of a conduit because it is used as a means of transport. Or consider the series of tubes metaphor coined by Senator Ted Stevens. Like a highway, a tube is a conduit that is used for the transportation of various things (usually, liquids and gases) from one place to another and is therefore mappable onto the global computer network as its source concept.

In addition to being a conduit—a highway or a series of tubes where information travels from one place to another—the Internet is also a container where information is stored. Not accidentally, the Internet is often called an *archive* or a *library*: Both terms are hyponyms of *container*. Also, it is interesting to note that we often speak of *uploading* or *posting something on the Internet*, even though in reality this is never taking place. Thus in strict technical terms, the Internet is "a network of geographically distributed machines connected via wires" (Maglio and Matlock 1999: 157). Hence, when speaking of *uploading* or *posting on the Internet*, we can only refer to transferring data to a provider's machine (e.g., provider of a video-sharing service like YouTube) which via wires is connected to other users' machines. However, *uploading on the Internet* suggests that the Internet has a container of its own different from the provider's machine to whom we send data which, we think, are being *uploaded on the Internet*.

Finally, the prosthesis metaphor highlights "the reach-extending capacity of the Internet" which "allows individuals to extend their limbs and senses great distances to connect with other people and databases" (Markham 2003: online). Linguistically, the prosthesis metaphor seems to have left traces in the names of some Web browsers (e.g., *Explorer*, *Safari*) as well as in the term *browser* itself (even though this connection is less obvious than between *conduit* and *highway*, and *container* and *archive*). Indeed, a Web browser is an extension of our computers' "senses and limbs," for it is namely a Web browser that allows them (and thus us) to *browse* through Web pages. It is namely a Web browser that enables us to *explore* Web sites that are located on servers in different countries of the world—a trip which can be not less exciting than a real-life *safari*.

Closely related to the three tool metaphors is the metaphor THE INTERNET IS A PLACE. Thus, with the exception of the prosthesis metaphor, all other tool metaphors seem to be place metaphors as well: A highway, for example, is not only a means of transport but a place "populated" by cars, drivers, maintenance workers, road signs, etc. Likewise, a library is not only a container for books, but a work*place* for librarians. Other examples include *agora, electronic frontier, empyrean realm, global village, ocean*, etc.—in other words, the majority (if not all) other Internet metaphors. All these expressions denote a place and can therefore be considered linguistic realizations of the super master metaphor THE INTERNET IS A PLACE.

Like container metaphors, place metaphors are "wrong" metaphors since in reality the Internet is, of course, not a place but, as just said, a "network of geographically distributed machines connected via wires." Thus when we speak of, e.g., *visiting a Web site* (which implies that a Web site is a *place* to which we or our computers *go*), neither we nor our computers move anywhere. Instead, we only "send a request for information to the provider of the Web site, and the provider sends back data: the Web page itself" (Lemley 2002: 6).

The issue of Internet super master metaphors is also discussed in a recent article by Porto Requejo (2007) who, like Markham, argues that one of such metaphors is THE INTERNET IS A PLACE. According to Porto Requejo, this is "the most extended and productive metaphor" (p. 199) which can be divided into multiple sub-metaphors. For example, THE INTERNET IS A CITY (e.g. *type the address of the Web site you want to visit*), THE INTERNET IS A SEA (e.g. *here are some safety tips for surfing the net*), THE INTERNET IS THE OUTER SPACE (e.g., *we encourage young Internauts to explore cyberspace*), THE INTERNET IS A CLUB (e.g. *you can join discussions, play games, meet people, etc.*), etc. (p. 200).

In a similar way, Gehring (2004) suggests that the main Internet super master metaphor is THE INTERNET IS A SPACE. (The difference between *space* and *place* is that the latter is usually a space filled with something, whereas the former connotes emptiness, e.g., *the spaces between words*, *the architect left space in front of the building*, etc.) But, unlike Markham and Porto Requejo who only assert that THE INTERNET IS A PLACE, Gehring attempts to explain why so many spatial concepts serve as source domains for the target domain INTERNET. According to Gehring, THE INTERNET IS A SPACE because THE INTERNET IS **NOT** A SPACE. That is, the Internet lacks space, but since the concept of space is so important for language users, spatial metaphors linguistically compensate the absence of space (p. 51).

This is a very interesting explanation which, however, fails to answer the following questions: Why do we need this metaphorical compensation for the loss of space? Why can we not accept the fact that the Internet has no space? Why do we speak of *visiting a Web site*, *going to a Web page*, *surfing the Web*, etc., if, from the technical point of view, the idea that the Internet is a space where we or our computers move from one Web site to another is "not only wrong but faintly ludicrous" (Lemley 2002: 5)?

As can be inferred from Woiskunski (2001: 307-308), the answer to this question is that the Internet has always been analogized to *spaces of a different dimension* such as, e.g., seas, oceans, outer space, etc.—spaces unpopulated by human beings and therefore attracting them (i.e., people have always wanted to explore these spaces). Accordingly, the conceptualization of the Internet as ocean, empyrean realm, outer space, etc. (which is linguistically realized by, e.g., the use of *surf*, *cruise*, and *navigate* to refer to movement on the Web as well as by such terms as *cybernaut*, *Explorer*, etc.) can be seen as an attempt to sublimate the desire of entering these spaces. Or, as Woiskunski puts it, "cyber-navigation and surfing the Web are metaphorical continuations of the very old yearning for travelling" (p. 307, my translation).

But all this does not account for the fact that the Internet is analogized to multiple place metaphors. That is, in addition to being AN OCEAN, AN EMPYREAN REALM, OUTER SPACE, etc., the Internet is also A CITY, A HIGHWAY, A LIBRARY, etc.—places which can hardly be considered places of a different dimension.

So, how do we then explain the use of these concepts as Internet source domains and why do we use motion verbs (*go*, *visit*, etc.) talking about retrieving

Web pages? The linguistic answer to these questions is that many Web sites are metaphorized as places in the real-world. For example, we have online shops, banking institutions (which can be accessed via online banking), chat rooms, online libraries and archives, universities, and some other places. Accordingly, if WEB SITES YOU RETRIEVE ARE PLACES IN THE REAL-WORLD, then RETRIEVING THESE WEB SITES IS VISITING OR GOING TO THESE PLACES. (This is an entailment of the source concept A PLACE IN THE REAL-WORLD.) Likewise, if THE INTERNET IS A COLLECTION OF REAL-LIFE PLACES, then the INTERNET IS A SPACE since the existence of a place presupposes the existence of space.

As for spaces of a different dimension, the linguistic grounding of these metaphors is, of course, not our yearning for travelling but certain connotations that the Internet shares with these concepts. For example, the connotation "immenseness/boundlessness" that the Internet shares with seas and oceans. Or "relative unexploredness" that the Internet of the early 1990s used to share with the outer space.

2.2. Web 2.0

Linguistically, the term *Web 2.0* is, first of all, an example of a semi-phraseme (Mel'čuk 1995: 182), i.e., a phrase or a poly-morphemic word whose overall meaning includes the literal meaning of one its constituents, whereas the other constituent denotes a concept which it does not denote in other environments. A good example of a semi-phraseme is *black coffee* whose meaning "served without milk or cream" (American Heritage Dictionary) includes the meaning of the constituent *coffee* but not of *black*: The defining characteristic of black coffee is not black color but the absence of milk or cream. Of course, it is clear that the meaning "served without milk or cream" is metonymically related to the meaning "black": With the exception of some particular coffee brands (e.g., Nescafe Gold), the absence of milk will always result in black color. Nevertheless, the meaning "without added milk or cream" is a non-standard meaning of *black* which can only be found in the collocation *black coffee*. (Even in a very similar collocation *black tea*, *black* does not refer to the absence of milk or cream but to the full fermentation of tea leaves.)

In a similar way, the meaning of *Web 2.0* can be said to include the meaning of the constituent *Web* but not of *2.0*:

Web 2.0
Web 2.0 is a trend in the use of World Wide Web technology and web design that aims to facilitate creativity, information sharing, and, most notably, collaboration among users. These concepts have led to the development and evolution of web-based communities and hosted services, such as social-networking sites, wikis, blogs, and folksonomies (the practice of categorizing content through tags). Although the term suggests a new version of the

World Wide Web, it does not refer to an update to any technical specifications, but to changes in the ways software developers and end-users use the internet.
http://www.stiltonstudios.net/glossary.htm

Web 2.0
A term coined by O'Reilly Media in 2004 to describe a second generation of the web. This describes more user participation, social interaction and collaboration with the use of blogs, wikis, social networking and folksonomies.
http://www.webdesignseo.com/blogging-terms/web-20-terms.php

Web 2.0
A term that refers to a supposed second generation of Internet-based services. These usually include tools that let people collaborate and share information online, such as social networking sites, wikis, communication tools, and folksonomies.
http://mytooltest.blogspot.com/

Given these definitions, it can be argued that the term *Web 2.0* means "second generation of the Web or Web-based services." That "second generation" cannot be the standard meaning of *2.0* has nothing to do with the fact that the numbers *2.0* cannot verbalize the concept "generation." (Neither *2* nor *0* contain the meaning "generation.") The point here is that the constituent *2.0* implies that Web 2.0 is a new software version of the World Wide Web that was released in 2004. This impression arises because the practice of assigning new numbers to a new version of the same software is a hallmark of the process of *software versioning*. For example, currently I browse the Web using Internet Explorer, version 7.0. But recently, Microsoft has released the version 8.0. The number before the period (e.g., *7* in *7.0*) is called *major* (or *major number*); the first number after the period—*minor* (or *minor number*). The increase of the major number symbolizes a major revision of a software; the increase of the minor—that only minor changes have been introduced. Accordingly, *2.0* in *Web 2.0* suggests that in 2004 there took place a release of the new software version of the Internet that was downloaded and installed by all (or at least a very large number of) Internet users.

However, as can be inferred from the above definitions of Web 2.0, the term *Web 2.0* was coined as a cover term for changes in the use of the existing Internet technology, not in the technology itself. (As is explicitly stated in one of the definitions, "although the term suggests a new version of the World Wide Web, it does not refer to an update to any technical specifications, but to changes in the ways software developers and end-users use the Internet.") This does not mean that there have been no technical innovations. Consider, for example, RSS (Really Simple Syndication/Rich Site Summary)—technology allowing users to subscribe to often-updated Web sites—which O'Reilly (2005) describes as "the most significant advance in the fundamental architecture of the Web." Nonetheless, the (linguistic) focus of the term *Web 2.0* is not on technology but on new Web-based services such as social networks, folksonomies, and wikis.

2.2.1. Web 2.0 genres

In the following, I will briefly describe what can be considered genres or socio-technical modes of Web 2.0. As defined by Herring (2007: 3), socio-technical modes are technologically-defined subtypes of computer-mediated communication such as, e.g., Internet Relay Chat (IRC), Usenet, e-mail, etc. Proceeding from this definition, Web 2.0 can be classified into at least four socio-technical modes: (1) social networks/social networking Web sites, (2) social bookmarks/social bookmarking Web sites, (3) blogging services, and (4) video- and photo-sharing services.

Social networking Web sites (SNSs) are services like MySpace, Facebook, hi5, Bebo, StudiVZ, etc., where users can keep in touch with already-friends and -acquaintances and/or make new ones by visiting other users' member profiles (i.e., personalized users' pages containing a user's description, photos and videos, etc.) and initiating a contact by sending a friend request (i.e., asking the recipient to add them to her/his friends list).

Social bookmarking Web sites (SBs) are services like Delicious, Furl, StumbleUpon, Digg, etc., allowing users to bookmark Web pages online (i.e., in their SBs' accounts) in order to access them on any computer connected to the Internet. In addition, SB users can search for content bookmarked by other users. (This is, by the way, the reason why SBs are called *social bookmarks*.)

Blogging services are services like LiveJournal, Blogger, Blogster, Windows Live Spaces, etc., where users post blog entries, i.e., texts, photos, and videos which are displayed in a reverse chronological order (i.e., beginning with the latest post).

Finally, the term *video-and photo-sharing services* is self-explaining: These are Web sites like YouTube, Veoh, Flickr, Photobucket, etc., hosting users' photos and videos.

As for folksonomies and wikis which are also often referred to as hallmarks of Web 2.0, it is important to emphasize that these are not genres but *practices* associated with Web 2.0 services of various genres.

Let us start with folksonomies. As was mentioned in the Introduction, the defining characteristic of a folksonomic Web site is the practice of collaborative tagging whereby users assign keywords of their own choice to the content which they would like to make findable for other users. A good example of a folksonomic Web site is the SB Delicious where users are required to tag a Web page which they want to bookmark. But apart from Delicious and some other SBs, tagging also occurs on photo- and video-sharing services like YouTube and Flickr where users tag photos and videos, a number of blogging sites like Live-

Journal where users tag blog posts, social music platforms like Last.fm where users tag music items; etc.

Similarly, wiki is not a genre of a wiki Web site like Wikipedia or Wikibooks but a Web site which can be edited by any Internet user. (Or, being more exact, wiki is, first of all, the software enabling the creation of such a Web site.) Accordingly, the genre of a wiki Web site depends on the content which it contains. For example, the genre of Wikipedia is encyclopedia. Wikibooks is a collection of textbooks. PenguinWiki is a novel that was collaboratively written by Internet users.

2.3. Web 2.0 metaphors: Preliminaries

Since the term *Web 2.0* does not refer to any significant changes in the technology of the World Wide Web, it is clear that Web 2.0 should not differ from Web 1.0 with regard to either master metaphors in the sense of Gozzi (1994a: 321) or true master metaphors/super master metaphors in the CTM sense. Indeed, like the Internet of 1990s-early 2000s, the Internet of the mid-late 2000s can be referred to as *information superhighway*, *cyberspace*, *global village*, etc.:

> 10 Speed Bumps on the **Information Superhighway**
> Search Engine Journal - **Feb 25, 2008**
> www.searchenginejournal.com/10-speed-bumps-on-the-information- superhighway/6418
>
> **Cyberspace** poses new war threat
> San Diego Union Tribune - **Mar 4, 2008**
> http://www.signonsandiego.com/uniontrib/20080304/news_1n4war.html
>
> The Guardian - **Jun 7, 2007**... Today the Internet is ubiquitous and to all intents and purposes we live in the information age. The **global village** hasn't healed the division of nations, class and culture or marked the birth of a new humanistic civilisation.
> http://www.guardian.co.uk/technology/2007/jun/07/guardianweeklytechnologysection.it

Of course, this does not mean that our conceptualization of the Internet has undergone no changes. As argued by Blavin and Cohen (2002), the history of the Internet can be divided into three periods—(1) early 1990s-mid 1990s; (2) mid 1990s-late 1990s; and (3) late 1990s-present day—each of which is characterized by a particularly pervasive metaphorical structure.

During the early 1990s, it was the metaphor THE INTERNET IS A CONDUIT whose main linguistic realization was the term *information superhighway*. The reason for this is that during this period the Internet was chiefly used for the transfer of information by means of the electronic mail. (According to Blavin and Cohen (p. 269), e-mail is the "paradigmatic instantiation" of the conduit metaphor.)

In the mid 1990s, many Internet users got acquainted with the global computer network through Web browsers such as Netscape Navigator and Internet Explorer (p. 257). As a result of this, the focus of the Internet has shifted from e-mail to cyberspace (or, being exact, to the Web which was metaphorized as *cyberspace*)—a novel space which was then believed to be remarkably different from all other spaces. It is the year 1996 when John Perry Barlow, the founder of the Electronic Frontier Foundation, writes his famous *Declaration of the Independence of Cyberspace* where he argues that the Internet should not be regulated by traditional territorial governments because Cyberspace does not lie within their borders.

Finally, in the late 1990s, as a consequence of the increased ubiquity of the Internet, the novel space metaphor was replaced by the metaphor THE INTERNET IS REAL SPACE—space that is not "hermetically sealed from the real world," but space that can be "interfered with, trespassed upon, or divided up into holdings similar to real property" (Blavin and Cohen 2002: 280).

But what about Web 2.0? Since the defining characteristic of a Web 2.0 site is user-generated content, it is not surprising that Web 2.0 is often described as a *platform* for such content (O'Reilly 2005). But *platform* is just another place metaphor, for as defined by, e.g., the American Heritage Dictionary, a platform is "a place, means, or opportunity for public expression of opinion."

As for features attributed to this platform, Web 2.0 can, first of all, be described as *unreal world*:

> Narcissists also tend to have more contacts on **Facebook**, and because of that, any given Facebook user is likely to have more narcissist friends **online** than they would in the **real world**.
> http://tinyurl.com/cdfe9r

> What happens if **MySpace** came to **real life**??? Would making friends still be as easy? You HAVE to watch this video to the END!!! Truly Hilarious!!!
> http://tinyurl.com/c9cfwa

As illustrated by these examples, the terms *real world* and *real life* are (still) used as cover terms for everything that does not involve the use of the Internet. Accordingly, if NOT USING A WEB 2.0 SERVICE LIKE MYSPACE AND FACEBOOK IS BEING IN THE REAL-WORLD, then WEB 2.0 IS AN UNREAL WORLD. At the same time, however, WEB 2.0 is simultaneously REAL WORLD since everything you do on the Internet in the Web 2.0 era may have consequences in the "real world." For example, SNSs are often described as *carrier killers* because many employers regularly check their employees' and job applicants' member profiles on services like MySpace and Facebook. But neither THE INTERNET AS UNREAL WORLD not the opposite of it are metaphors that specifically apply to Web 2.0. Both had emerged long before the rise of Web 2.0 services.

Given these facts, the focus of this study is on neither master metaphors like *information superhighway* nor super master metaphors like THE INTERNET IS A CONDUIT, but on metaphorical expressions associated with some of the Web 2.0 services. Part 2 is devoted to four metaphors—*sign up, profile, friend*, and *poke (five, smile, etc.)*—that are characteristic of most SNSs. Part 3 deals with the terms *tag, subscribe*, and *channel*—terms that can often be found in the context of folksonomic Web sites.

Each chapter represents an independent case study that aims (1) to establish what the term under analysis stands for (i.e., describe it from the referential point of view); (2) to describe the structure of the conceptual metaphor which the term realizes linguistically. This means, to establish which elements of the metaphor's source domain map/do not map onto the target domain and why; (2) to analyze its intensional semantics (i.e., what the term under consideration means/which concept it signifies); and, when possible, (3) to find out whether there are any differences in how the term is understood by the creators and users of these services who are "forced" to use it by the creators.

All metaphors chosen for these case studies have a very low degree of metaphoricity because (1) all these expressions realize conceptual metaphors of the electronic journal type, i.e., metaphors characterized by systematic ontological correspondences between their source and target domains; and because (2) these expressions do not fulfill the additional naming requirement: each of these terms is a primary expression for the concept which it denotes. The reason for this choice is that metaphors of the electronic journal type are usually not consciously recognized as metaphors and therefore attract much less scholarly attention than non-systematic metaphors of the firewall type and expressions like *information superhighway, electronic frontier, agora*, etc., which fulfill the additional naming requirement.

PART 2 SOCIAL NETWORKS

3. Registration

The focus of this chapter will be on the registration metaphor which has been well-known since the early years of the Internet. (That is, already in the 1990s Web users were required to register for a number of services including Web-based e-mail, Web forums, IRC, etc.)

At the level of frames—i.e., conceptual structures describing "a particular type of situation, object, or event and the participants and props involved in it" (Ruppenhofer et al. 2006: online)—the concept of registration seems to be integrated into the frame of BECOMING A MEMBER OF A GROUP. That is, whenever we register for something both in real-life and on the Internet, we always become members of the group of people who register(ed) for the same thing as us. For example, when we register at a conference, we become members of the group of conference participants. When we check in at a hotel (which is a form of registration), we become members of the group of hotel guests. When we sign up for an SNS like MySpace and Facebook, we become members of the group of users of these services; etc.

As described by FrameNet, the BECOMING A MEMBER frame consists of two core elements (i.e., elements instantiating "conceptually necessary component[s] of a frame" and thereby "making the frame unique and different from other frames," Ruppenhofer et al. ibid.):

(1) **Group**, i.e., a socially-constructed entity composed of members; and
(2) **New member**, i.e., a person who joins the group.

as well as of 12 non-core or peripheral elements (i.e., elements that provide additional information describing the main event). For example,

(1) **Time** (which identifies the time when the new member joins the group);
(2) **Place** (which identifies the place where the joining occurs);
(3) **Role** (the capacity or role in which the new member is placed upon joining the group);
(4) **Manner** (which specifies how the new member joins the group); etc.

In the context of real-life groups, the idea of becoming a member is verbalized by multiple expressions including *sign up* (e.g., *sign up for yoga classes*), *register* (e.g., *register for the draft*), *enlist* (e.g., *enlist in the navy*), *enroll* (e.g., *enroll at a college*), *enter* (e.g., *enter Parliament*), *join* (e.g., *join a club*), etc. In the context of SNSs and other Web-based groups, the preference is, however, usually given to the phrasal verb *sign up*, whereas the process of signing up is most commonly referred to as *registration*.

Given what we said about the BECOMING A MEMBER frame, there arises the question of whether the terms *sign up* and *registration* can be considered metaphorical expressions if they convey one and the same idea of becoming a member of a socially-defined group when used to refer to an SNS like MySpace and Facebook and a real-life group like university. What is the semantic difference between *sign up* in *sign up for Facebook* and *sign up* in *sign up for a university course*?

To answer this question, let us, first of all, consider the German term *immatrikulieren* "matriculate" which verbalizes the concept of registration on StudiVZ (www.studivz.net), a popular SNS for university students in German-speaking countries. In contrast to *sign up*, *immatrikulieren* is an expression which German speakers consciously recognize as a metaphor. Linguistically, this is reflected in, e.g., the (frequent) use of quotation marks accompanying *immatrikulieren* when preceded or followed by *StudiVZ*:

> Es müssen also täglich mehr als 21.000 Studenten bereit sein bei StudiVZ und Co. zu "immatrikulieren". Wow... Was für eine Zahl. Was für Dimensionen.
> [More than 21.000 students must be ready to "matriculate" at StudiVZ and Co. every day. Wow... What a number. What a dimension.]
> http://www.blogwave.de/studivz-braucht-640000-neue-mitglieder-pro-monat.html

It is clear that if *immatrikulieren* meant "matriculate," quotation marks would be out of place here since *immatrikulieren* is the term which on StudiVZ is used to denote registration.

But why is *immatrikulieren* (and not *sign up*) perceived as a metaphor? This question arises because, like *sign up*, *matriculate* also conveys the idea of becoming a member of a socially-defined group composed of members. (Thus a person who matriculates at a university becomes a member of the group of university students.)

The CTM answer to this question is that some of our knowledge about the source domain MATRICULATION IN THE REAL-WORLD do not apply to the target domain SIGNING UP FOR STUDIVZ. First of all, this refers to the fact that in the real-world we can only matriculate at a university (not at any other group!), and StudiVZ is obviously not a university but (only) a Web service designed to be used by university students. Apart from this, traditional matriculation involves admission offices that always check the fulfillment of universities' admission requirements. By contrast, StudiVZ has "admission requirements"—e.g., its members are supposed to be currently-enrolled university students or alumni—but a very bad "admission office" that does not seem to care much whether new members fulfill them. Thus Internet users "applying for" StudiVZ membership are not required to provide their current or former Student IDs in order to be "admitted" to StudiVZ. Instead, they only have to fill out a very short registration form containing seven questions: "First name," "Last name," "Date of birth," "Sex," "University," "E-mail," and "Password."

The *immatrikulieren*-example is another good illustration of what was said about the degree of metaphoricity in chapter 2: The less elements of the metaphor's source domain have correspondences in the target domain, the greater the metaphoricity. Important is also the fact that in the case of *immatrikulieren*, the just named epistemic differences between the source domain MATRICULATION IN THE REAL-WORLD and the target domain SIGNING UP FOR STUDIVZ concern one of the two core elements of the BECOMING A MEMBER frame, Group: As aforementioned, many of our knowledge about universities (as a group) do not apply to StudiVZ. Also, it must be noted that *immatrikulieren* fulfills the additional naming requirement: In German, the concept of signing up for an SNS or any other Web-based service is usually verbalized by *registrieren* "register," not *immatrikulieren*.

Taking all this into account, let us now proceed to *sign up*. Like "matriculating" at StudiVZ, signing up for Facebook exhibits an important difference from registering in the real-world. Retaining the university terminology, this difference can be described as absence versus presence of "admission offices." What is meant by this is that one of the key characteristics of real-life groups which register their members is that new membership must always be approved of by one or more already-members of that group chosen for this particular purpose. Consider, for example, the already mentioned universities' admission offices that are entitled to decide who will be allowed to join the University group as students, i.e., be able to *enroll/register/sign up* for a university course. Likewise, we cannot check in at a hotel—that is, join the Hotel group as hotel guests—without being approved of as hotel guests by a hotel clerk. Other similar examples include signing up for a military service, a yoga class, an audition, etc.

Summarizing: When registering for a membership in the above mentioned real-world groups, we are often confronted with a number of "admission requirements," e.g., possessing a university-entrance qualification, having enough money to pay for a hotel room, being physically able to serve in the army or take part in a yoga class, etc. Particularly important is also that these and other similar requirements cannot be unfulfilled since universities, hotels, armies, and groups alike employ people—admission office staff, hotel clerks, recruitment center workers, etc.—whose specific task is to monitor the admission process, i.e., check whether new members fulfill the "admission requirements."

As for SNSs like MySpace and Facebook, the situation is very similar to that of StudiVZ. These services have "admission requirements"—e.g., their users are supposed to be of a certain age as well to submit truthful and accurate information when filling out a registration form—

[Facebook] is intended solely for users who are thirteen (13) years of age or older, and users of the Site under 18 who are currently in high school or college. Any registration by, use of or access to the Site by anyone under 13, or by anyone who is under 18 and not in high school or college, is unauthorized, unlicensed and in violation of these Terms of Use.
http://www.facebook.com/terms.php?ref=pf

By using the MySpace Services, you represent and warrant that (a) all registration information you submit is truthful and accurate; (b) you will maintain the accuracy of such information; (c) you are 13 years of age or older; and (d) your use of the MySpace Services does not violate any applicable law or regulation.
http://www.myspace.com/index.cfm?fuseaction=misc.terms

—but no "admission offices" (or, as was observed in connection with StudiVZ, they have very bad "admission offices" that do not check whether new members fulfill these requirements).

A well-known consequence of the absence of "admission offices" is the problem of fake problems (of, e.g., famous people) which can be easily found on almost any SNS.

Screenshot 1. Fake profiles on Facebook

In contrast, real-life groups like universities and hotels do not know this problem. Indeed, we can hardly imagine a student registering for a university course as Osama bin Laden (unless his name is identical with that of the world's most famous terrorist) or a hotel guest identifying himself as Vladimir Putin (unless his name is also Vladimir Putin). The explanation for this is that "admission office" is one of the obligatory participants of the situation REGISTRATION IN THE REAL-WORLD. That is, being aware of the existence of "admission offices," we are also aware that an attempt to deliberately violate admission requirements (e.g., register with false names) will inevitably lead to legal prosecution or other similar negative consequences. Conversely, SNS users know that services like MySpace and Facebook do not have "admission offices." Accordingly, they can easily violate "admission requirements" without the fear of being prosecuted.

In CTM terms, the situation which we are dealing with here can be described as a partial ontological mapping of the source concept TRADITIONAL REGISTRATION onto the target concept SNS REGISTRATION: Whereas the entities "group" and "new member" equally apply to both the source and the target, the element "admission office" was deliberately not mapped by SNS creators from the source concept TRADITIONAL REGISTRATION onto the target concept SNS REGISTRATION in order to expedite the latter. (Just imagine a hypothetical SNS like StudiVZ which, like a real-life group, checks whether new members fulfill its admission requirements: That is, first of all, users send their student IDs and passports to the provider of a site and only then are allowed to sign in to their accounts. I assume, no one will sign up for such a service.) It is namely this non-mapping of "admission offices" that allows us to consider *sign up* and *register* referential metaphors: In the context of SNSs, these terms refer to a process different from the prototypical real-life registration and therefore qualify as metaphors from the extensional point of view.

As for the intensional perspective, *sign up* is not a metaphor because the concept which it signifies in, e.g., *sign up for Facebook* is not different from that of *sign up* in *sign up for a university course*. According to WordNet, *sign up* (in the latter context) means "join a club, an activity, etc. with the intention to join or participate." According to the American Heritage Dictionary— "to agree to be a participant or recipient by signing one's name; enlist." According to Merriam-Webster Unabridged —"to join a working force or an organization or scheme or accept an obligation by signing a contract."

Now, let us consider whether these definitions apply to *sign up* when used in the context of SNS registration. The obvious answer to this question is yes. Just as a high school graduate can *join* a university by *signing up* for a university course, so an Internet user can *join* an SNS by *registering* for it. Just as a college student who *signs up* for a university course *enlists* her/himself as a participant of that course, so an Internet user who *signs up* for an SNS *enlists* her/himself as a participant of that SNS. Just as a college student who *signs up* for a university course *accepts a number of obligations* (e.g., to regularly attend classes, to do homework, etc.), so an Internet user who *signs up* for an SNS *accepts an obligation* to use that SNS in accordance with its terms of use.

That the absence of "admission offices" has not changed the intensional meaning of *sign up* is most likely due to the fact that despite being an obligatory participant of the situation REGISTRATION IN THE REAL-WORLD, "admission office" is not a core element of the BECOMING A MEMBER frame. Instead, it is part of the non-core element Manner which, as stated in the beginning of the chapter, specifies the manner in which new members join a group. For example, I signed up for a university course *by sending the application form to the university's admission office which, having established that I fulfill all the admission requirements, accepted me as a student.* Or, I signed up for Facebook *by filling out a registration form containing the questions "Name," "Password," etc., and then confirming the registration by clicking at the confirmation link which I received in an e-mail that was automatically sent to me by Facebook.*

As for the core elements, it is clear that signing up for Facebook does not differ from signing up in real-life because, in contrast to *matriculate*, *sign up* collocates with various real-life groups (e.g., university, army, yoga class, etc.), so that the use of *sign up* in the context of Facebook does not evoke the sense of inappropriateness which *immatrikulieren* does when used in the StudiVZ context. That is, one cannot (literally) matriculate at StudiVZ because StudiVZ is not a university. But one can sign up for Facebook because one can sign up for almost any group.

4. Profile

After registration SNS users are expected to start editing their member profiles. Editing a profile is similar to filling out a registration form in that in both cases users are requested to provide some personal information. However, whereas filling out a registration form is one of the "admission requirements" that must be necessarily fulfilled by anyone who wants to join an SNS, editing a profile is an optional activity that can be skipped and returned to anytime the user wishes. Another difference relates to the number of questions which users are supposed to answer when filling out a registration form and editing a profile. While the former contains a relatively small number of (obligatory) questions—typically, "Full name," "Date of birth," "E-mail address," and "Password"—the latter includes numerous questions—e.g., "Hometown," "Marital status," "Education," "Political views," "Hobbies," etc.—which users can leave unanswered if they do not want to share these information with other users.

Like *sign up* and *registration*, *profile* is hardly a Web 2.0 terminological innovation: Profiles have been created and edited since the early years of the Internet by users of such genuinely Web 1.0 services as Web-based e-mail, IRC, Internet forums, etc. However, as will be shown below, SNS member profiles are characterized by a number of features that were untypical of profiles in the Web 1.0 era.

4.1. Internet profiles versus traditional profiles

But to begin with, let us, first of all, have a brief look at the major differences between traditional profiles (PROFILES1) and users' member profiles (PROFILES2). For this purpose, let us consider the profile of the U.S. Secretary of State Hillary Rodham Clinton that was published on the NYT Web site in November 2007 (when Hillary Clinton was a U.S. senator and a 2008 presidential candidate) and the profile of the ICQ user Blackcat (pp. 35-36).

The two profiles resemble each other in that they aim to provide the most basic information—name, date of birth, hometown, employment, etc.—about the person they describe. Accordingly, the core of the intensional semantics of *profile*—the meanings "biographical sketch" (WordNet), "a concise biographical sketch" (Merriam-Webster Online), "a short descriptive article about someone" (Compact Oxford English Dictionary), etc.—can be said to be equally characteristic of both PROFILES1 and PROFILES2. At the same time, it is clear that the two profiles differ in many essential respects. First of all, whereas the NYT profile represents Hillary Clinton with her real name and photograph, the ICQ profile does not disclose the user's real-life identity: *Blackcat* is most likely a username (not the user's true name!), and the animated picture of a black cat that can also

Screenshot 2. NYT profile of Hillary Clinton

Hillary Rodham Clinton

Biography
Full Name: Hillary Rodham Clinton
Party: Democratic
Political Office: U.S. Senator from New York; elected 2000; reelected 2006
Business/Professional Experience: Partner, Rose Law Firm (Little Rock, AR), 1979-1992
Date of Birth: October 26, 1947
Place of Birth: Chicago, IL
Education: B.A., Wellesley College, 1969; J.D. Yale University, 1973
Spouse: former President Bill Clinton; married 1975
Children: daughter, Chelsea; born 1980
Religion: Methodist
Home: Chappaqua, NY
Campaign Web Site: www.hillaryclinton.com

Screenshot 3. Blackcat's profile on ICQ (www.icq.com)

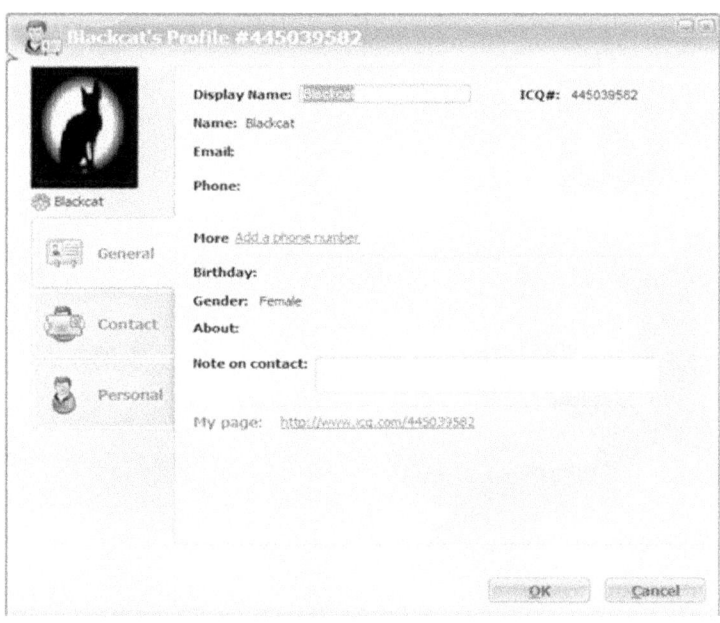

Screenshot 3. Blackcat's profile on ICQ (cont.)

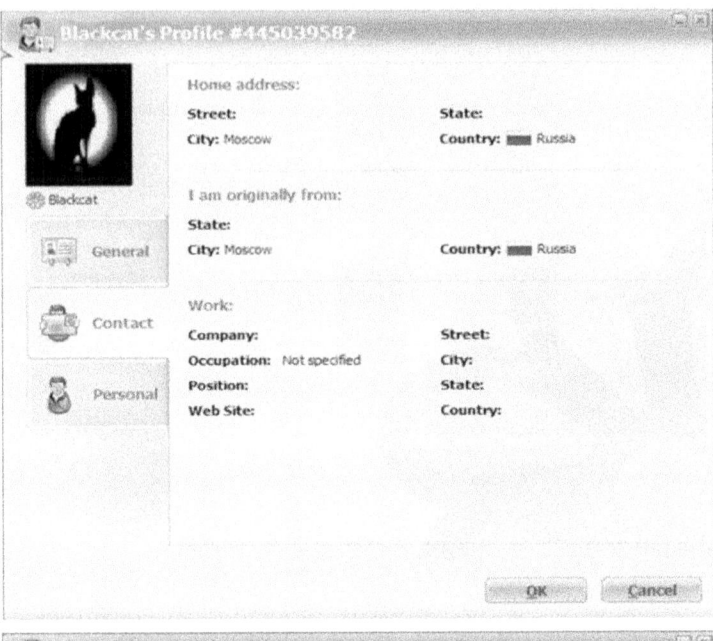

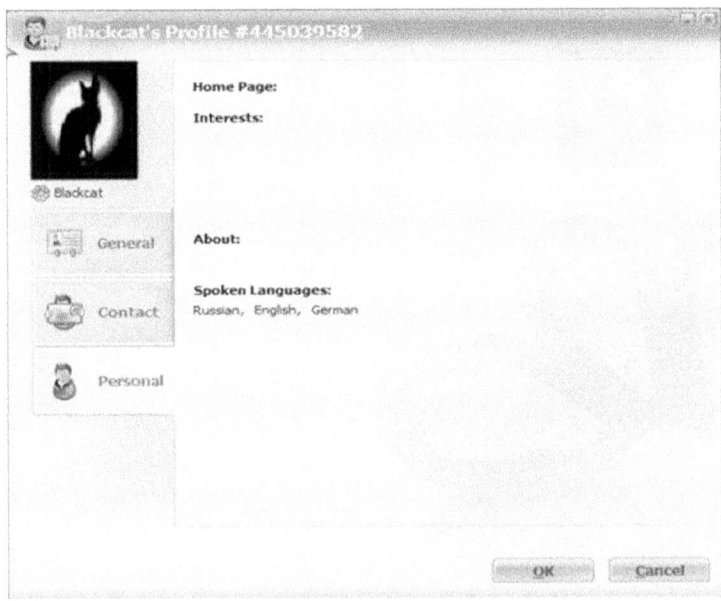

be found there is an avatar that Blackcat uses to represent herself to other people on the network.

Another fundamental difference relates to the amount of information that can be found in these two profiles. Undeniably, the NYT profile contains much more information about Hillary Clinton than the ICQ profile about Blackcat: Whereas the former is indeed a short description of Hillary Clinton's life story that includes the usual biographical information such as full name, place/date of birth, education, career, marital status, etc., the latter can hardly be referred to as even a *very concise* biographical sketch. By telling that Blackcat is (1) female; (2) native-born resident of Moscow; (3) fluent in Russian, English, and German, the ICQ profile does not provide a single piece of information uniquely applicable to Blackcat—i.e., Blackcat is most likely not the only female Muscovite who speaks Russian, English, and German—and therefore cannot be considered a biography.

Another important difference between the two profiles can be described as presence versus absence of explicit empty fields. As mentioned in the beginning of this chapter, users of most Internet services are only encouraged but not required to fill out their member profiles. The consequence of this is that the overwhelming majority of PROFILES2 contain empty fields, i.e., unanswered questions such as, for example, "E-mail," "Birthday," "Occupation," "Interests," etc., on Blackcat's profile. Traditional profiles, by contrast, disallow empty fields. Thus, if we edit Hillary Clinton's NYT profile in the way Blackcat filled out her ICQ profile, it will no longer qualify as a profile worthy of being published in the NYT or any other traditional newspaper. More than that, we will not be able to use the word *profile* (let alone *biography*) referring to such a "profile," for it will contain too many explicit empty fields and therefore will not do what a profile is supposed to do: describe the profiled person.

In this regard, it is also worth mentioning that it is only PROFILES2 (but, as far as I can judge, not PROFILES1) that can be *empty profiles*:

Empty Profiles – The Curse of the Online Dating Website
http://tinyurl.com/dze5lj

The term *empty profile* can be considered *contradictio in adjecto* because if *profile* is defined as a description (which suggests that [+description] is one of the distinctive features of the concept PROFILE), then the absence of description (which is characteristic of empty profiles) should automatically terminate the situation BEING A PROFILE: That is, if there is no description, then the thing in question cannot be a profile. But, as just said, this is only true of traditional profiles which disallow explicit empty fields, whereas PROFILES2 qualify as *profiles* regardless of the degree of emptiness.

Finally, it must be observed that with the exception of fake profiles, the person described in PROFILE2 is always the author of that profile. For example, Blackcat is the author of Blackcat's profile.

In contrast, a traditional profile is usually not a self-description but a biographical sketch, i.e., a description of someone (usually famous person) written by someone else. For example, the NYT profile of Hillary Clinton was written by an NYT journalist, not by Hillary Clinton herself. Linguistically, this difference is reflected in the neologism *profile owner* that can only make sense in the context of PROFILE2.

> However, some developers have exploited this functionality to effectively spam a user's profile page box with ads that are only visible to profile visitors and not visible to the **profile owner**.
> http://tinyurl.com/c9za9x

For example, Blackcat can be called the *owner* of Blackcat's ICQ profile because (1) she is the author of this profile; and (2) she has the absolute power over it: She can edit it anytime she wants. Quite to the contrary, Hillary Clinton is not the owner of the NYT profile of Hillary Clinton because (1) she is not the author of this profile; and (2) she cannot edit it.

Summarizing: In the case of PROFILE2, we are also dealing with a non-mapping of some of our knowledge about the source domain TRADITIONAL PROFILE onto the target domain MEMBER PROFILE. As in the *registration*-example discussed in the previous chapter, it was the creators of IRC, Web forums, SNSs, etc., who have deliberately not mapped the obligatoriness of a more or less complete description of a profiled person from PROFILES1 onto PROFILES2 in order to enable users to have the full control over their member profiles—that is, share only those information which they want to share and be able to edit their profiles anytime they want—or, in other words, to make them *profile owners*.

Particularly important here is that in contrast to *sign up* whose intensional semantics has not "suffered" from the removal of "admission offices," the lexeme PROFILE2 does not signify the same concept as PROFILE1. Thus none of the previously mentioned dictionary definitions of PROFILE1—"biographical sketch," "a concise biographical sketch," "a short descriptive article about someone"—seem to yield an adequate description of the conceptual meaning of PROFILE2.

First of all, PROFILE2 cannot be equated with a biography since the person described in it is usually the author of a profile. More important, however, is the fact that many Internet profiles (e.g., Blackcat's profile) contain very little user-specific information and therefore can hardly be analogized to biographies. Hence, an attempt to redefine PROFILE2 as an autobiography does not seem to yield an accurate definition as well. Finally, even *description of a user* is not an entirely satisfactory definition since, given the possibility of fake profiles, we can never be sure that the information presented in PROFILE2 is indeed the description of the profile owner and not of anybody else.

The fact that PROFILE2 cannot be described in the same way as PROFILE1 confirms that the former does not have the same intensional meaning as the latter: PROFILE2 does not mean a "concise biography" but, as illustrated by the definitions below, "any information which users provide during registration":

Profile
Information about a user. A "profile" may contain details such as the users' name, hometown, interests, pictures, etc. Profiles are commonly used on social networking Web sites to help people get to know each other.
http://www.netlingo.com/word/profile.php

What Is a Profile?
A profile is the personal information you provided during registration.
https://www.gartner.com/6_help/site_help/SiteHelpProfile.jsp

What is a Profile?
A profile includes personal information you wish to share such as your web address or weblog address.
http://forums.microsoft.com/MSDN/languages/EN-US/docs/faq.aspx?siteid=1#8

Particularly interesting is also that all these definitions are answers to the question "What is a profile?" that can often be found among the so-called Frequently Asked Questions (FAQs). The mere existence of the question *What is a profile?* as an FAQ is another piece of linguistic evidence suggesting that the intensional semantics of PROFILE2 is not identical with that of PROFILE1. And at least some language users—i.e., providers of various Internet services whose users are required to create a profile as well as users of these services who *frequently asked this question*—are consciously aware of this fact. If this were not the case, *What is a profile?* would never become an FAQ.

Having established in which respects the intensional meaning of PROFILE2 is different from that of PROFILE1, we can also conclude that PROFILE2 is not a metaphor but a metonym of PROFILE1. Indeed, the semantic development undergone by *profile*—"concise biography" > "any information"—fulfills the within-domain mapping requirement of metonymy since both meanings can be seen as elements of one and the same conceptual domain INFORMATION. Thus PROFILE1 is usually said to mean "biography," i.e., "biographical and true information about the person whom it describes," whereas PROFILE2 means "any information"—i.e., both biographical (e.g., birthday) and non-biographical (e.g., homepage), true (e.g., real name) and untrue (e.g., username like *Blackcat*), etc.—that users can provide during registration or while editing a profile.

4.2. SNS profiles from the referential point of view

Having clarified the differences between PROFILES1 and PROFILES2 from both the extensional and the intensional points of view, we are now in a position to discuss the peculiarities of SNS profiles (PROFILES2_2.0). The two questions that will be addressed below are very similar to the questions that were discussed in the previous section. First of all, do PROFILES2_2.0 differ from PROFILES2_1.0, i.e., profiles created by users of Internet forums, IRC, and other similar Web 1.0 services? And second: If this is indeed the case, are these differences reflected in the intensional meaning of *profile*? That is, does the word *profile* signify a different concept when used to refer to PROFILES2_1.0 (e.g., Blackcat's profile) and PROFILES2_2.0 (i.e., SNS profiles)?

As an illustrative example of an SNS profile, let us consider another profile of Hillary Clinton—the one that can be found at MySpace. Below is the description of the profile yielded by the Google search engine when run for "Hillary Clinton MySpace":

MySpace.com – Hillary Clinton – 61– Female – Chappaqua, New York...
Official profile page for Hillary Clinton includes her weblog, blurbs, news clips, videos and comments from her MySpace friends.
www.myspace.com/hillaryclinton

Particularly interesting about the description is that it enables us to name the major difference between PROFILES2_2.0 and PROFILES2_1.0 even without visiting the Web page: None of the items which are enumerated there do we (usually) find in PROFILES2_1.0. Blackcat's profile, for example, does not contain the items "Weblog," "News clips," "Videos," and "Comments from friends."

Another interesting aspect is that the description above does not explicitly mention whether the profile includes a PROFILE2_1.0-like description of Hillary Clinton, i.e., biographical information, username, interests, e-mail address, etc. If this is not the case, we will have to admit that PROFILES2_2.0 have basically nothing in common with PROFILES2_1.0: Whereas the former consist of a variety of items including "Blog," "Videos," "News clips," etc., the latter can only include information describing the profile owner such as "Name," "Hometown," "Interests," "Pictures," etc. This will mean that PROFILE2_2.0 is not a polyseme but a homonym of PROFILE2_1.0. That is, the semantic relationship between the two senses, in this hypothetic case, can only have a homonymic character since the presumed intensional meaning of PROFILE2_2.0 ("variety of items such as "Blog," "Videos," "Comments from friends," etc.) does not share a single semantic feature with PROFILE2_1.0 ("information about a user"), so that the origin of the former could be traced to either metaphoric or metonymic extension of the latter. However, the probability of this scenario is rather low. Thanks to a number of studies on semantic change (e.g., Sperber 1923, Waldron 1979, Hughes 1988, Blank 1997, Traugott and Dasher 2002, Keller and Kirschbaum 2003, etc.), we know that meaning does not change in an entirely arbitrary fashion, as this could have been inferred from the Saussurean conception of a linguistic sign. Even lexical semantic change described by Hock (1986: 308) as "fuzzy, highly irregular and extremely difficult to predict" is regular in the sense that it is always based on either similarity (metaphor) or contiguity (metonymy) of senses. Knowing this, we can predict that the word *table*, for example, will never come to mean "sun" since the meaning "sun" can hardly be arrived at via metaphoric or metonymic extension of "table." Given this, it can be conjectured that (1) PROFILE2_2.0 is a polyseme of PROFILE2_1.0, i.e., the semantic relationship between them is similar to that between PROFILE1 and PROFILE2; as well as that (2) PROFILES2_2.0 include a PROFILE2_1.0-like description of the profile owner.

As for the question of why this is not explicitly mentioned in the description of Hillary Clinton's MySpace profile, the following explanations seem plausible. First of all, this may be due to *blurbs* (i.e., one of the terms enumerated in the above description) which on MySpace stands for the profile sections "About me" and "Who I'd like to meet"—sections where profile owners describe themselves as well as people whom they'd like to meet. It is obvious that "Personal information" is part of the extensional meaning of *blurbs*—the blurb "About me" is supposed to contain such information—and therefore does not need to be explicitly mentioned.

Another possible explanation is that Hillary Clinton is not an ordinary Internet user who signed up for MySpace just in order to communicate with other users of this popular SNS platform, but the U.S. Secretary of State as well as a former presidential candidate who used to utilize her MySpace profile for purposes other than social networking, e.g., campaigning, online fund-raising, etc. Accordingly, the focus of this profile is not on her biography but on items like "Blog," "Videos," "News clips," etc.

Finally, this can be attributed to the presumed Web users' unawareness of the above mentioned differences between PROFILES2_2.0 and PROFILES2_1.0. What is meant by this is that since Web 2.0 is a relatively new phenomenon, some Internet users may not know that SNS profiles contain such items as "Blog," "Videos," "Comments from friends," etc., which are untypical of traditional Internet profiles. At the same time, however, they do know that member profiles usually contain such items as "First name/Last name/Username," "Interests," "E-mail," etc., so that the information about these items can be easily omitted.

Anyway, Hillary Clinton's MySpace profile, in addition to the items enumerated in the above description, does, of course, contain what can be considered her PROFILE2_1.0-like description (see screenshot 4, next page).

42

Screenshot 4. Hillary Clinton's description on her MySpace profile

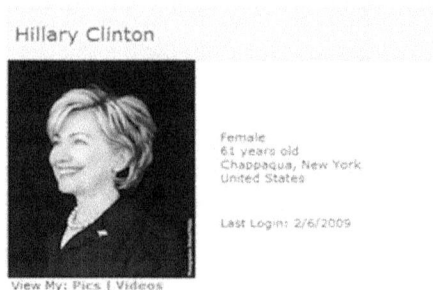

Concluding our discussion of the referential aspects of PROFILES2_2.0, it must finally be noted that there seems to be very little variation between different SNSs with respect to the structure of their member profiles. Thus, on (as far as I know) all SNSs, profiles contain a PROFILE2_1.0-like description of the profile owner, i.e., items like personal information (e.g., "Name," "Date of birth," "Hometown," etc.), contact information (usually in the form of hyperlinks, e.g., "Send a message," "Leave a comment," etc., enabling other users to contact the profile owner), users' interests and hobbies, and so on. Likewise, on all SNSs, member profiles contain "Friends":

Screenshot 5. Friends on hi5.com

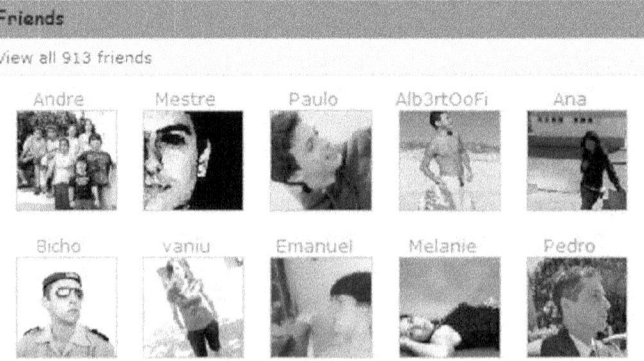

The elements "Friends" and "PROFILE2_1.0-like description" seem to be the necessary and sufficient criteria of PROFILE2_2.0-hood, i.e., the minimal requirements that a Web page must fulfill in order to be considered an SNS profile. As

for the latter, the presence of a PROFILE2_1.0-like description is necessary because it maps the intensional semantics of *profile*—the meaning "information about a user"—from PROFILES2_1.0 onto PROFILES2_2.0. Therefore, a Web page lacking such a description cannot be called a profile. Similarly, a page without "Friends" cannot be called an SNS profile because, as mentioned in chapter 2, the essence of online social networking is either keeping up with existing friends and acquaintances or making new ones by "friending" your friends' friends, i.e., visiting your friends' profiles and adding their friends to your own "Friends" section.

In addition to "Friends" and "PROFILE2_1.0-like description," the average SNS profile contains many other elements which, despite their seeming non-obligatoriness in terms of the necessary and sufficient criteria, nevertheless play an important role in the structure of an SNS profile. For example, the "Comments" section where profile visitors can leave public messages; the list of discussion groups and networks which the profile owner is a member of; numerous third-party applications such as, e.g., SuperFive on hi5 and SuperPoke on Facebook enabling users to send animated messages; and so on.

4.3. Intensional meaning

Having established in which respects PROFILES2_2.0 are different from PROFILES2_1.0, we can now proceed to the intensional semantics of *profile*. For this purpose, let us consider the following definitions of SNS profiles:

> Your Profile is **Your Space on the Web**, where you can describe yourself, hobbies and interests. You can even upload pics and write journals.
> http://collect.myspace.com/index.cfm?fuseaction=misc.about

> A MySpace profile is the **personal website** of a single user.
> http://web.archive.org/web/20080212044703/http://www.all4myspace.com/

> [A] Facebook profile is a **page on the internet** where you talk about yourself, your interests, favorite music, movies, books, your relationship status (single, dating, married...), and anything else you want to share, including your address, telephone number, and what classes you are taking for the semester.
> http://www.cbsnews.com/blogs/2007/08/07/couricandco/entry3143891.shtml

> Your profile is the **homepage of your website** and can be used for telling visitors about yourself.
> http://croftmiester.myfriendsreunited.com/?wci=faqs

Given these definitions, it appears that PROFILE2_2.0 has a different intensional meaning than PROFILE2_1.0: Whereas the latter is usually described as *information about a user*, the former is referred to as *page on the Internet*, *homepage*, *personal Web site*, *space*, etc., containing such information plus items like "Blog," "Photos and videos," "Comments from friends," etc. (It is clear from this that these meanings are polysemes since both of them contain the semantic component "description/information about a user.")

In connection with this finding, there arises the following question: How can it be that *profile*—the word meaning "description"—came to be referred as *page on the Internet*, *personal Web site*, *homepage*, *space*, etc.? At first glance, this may seem a rather trivial question: PROFILE2_2.0 is called a *Web page* because it has a physical location on the Internet which in English and in many other languages is conventionally called *Web page*. That PROFILE2_2.0 can also be referred to as a *Web site* follows from the fact that SNS profiles usually consist of more than one Web page. (And a Web site is a collection of interlinked Web pages!). Finally, in order to explain why an SNS profile is called a *space*, we need to recall that THE INTERNET IS A SPACE is one of the Internet super master metaphors which, to a very large extent, determines how we think and talk about the global computer network.

However, this line of argumentation will inevitably lead us to the wrong conclusion that "a page on the Internet/personal Web site/homepage/space" is not the intension but the *extension* of PROFILE2_2.0. In other words, the lexeme PROFILE2_2.0 does not really mean (i.e., signify the concept of) a personal Web site but only refers to it. (Likewise, it can be argued that PROFILE1 does not really mean "article" (even though the Compact Oxford English Dictionary defines it as a "short descriptive *article* about someone") but only refers to it since traditional profiles often have the form of a newspaper article.) But, as said above, this would be a wrong conclusion because it is mainly SNS profiles that are referred to as *Web pages*, whereas PROFILES2_1.0 are usually described as *information about a user*. Particularly interesting here is that this fact cannot be accounted for in terms of any actual differences between PROFILES2_2.0 and PROFILES2_1.0: Similar to the former, the latter often have a physical location on the Internet that could be called a *Web page* (but not a *Web site* because a PROFILE2_1.0-like description typically does not occupy more than one Internet page). Nevertheless, PROFILES2_1.0 are rarely called *Web pages*, let alone *Web sites*.

In addition to this, consider the term *profile page* which can denote both PROFILES2_2.0 and PROFILES2_1.0. Particularly interesting about this term is that during the last three years it underwent a dramatic increase in the frequency of use. Thus the search for "profile page" using Google News Archive Search—a research tool that allows to search across a "collection of historical archives including major newspapers [and] magazines, news archives and legal archives"—yields only 2060 results for the 1990s and 11500 results for 2005-2008. As far as the latter is concerned, *profile page* is predominantly used in the context of SNS Web sites such as MySpace, Facebook, hi5, Bebo, etc.

> Once registered, you set up your **Facebook profile page**. You can post your photo and personal information, such as your relationship status, political views, academic major and interests as well as your favorite movie, books, music and quotes.
> http://seacoastauction.com/2005news/11172005/it/73577.htm

> Companies have found that it is not easy to keep up with the online crowd. One of the first promotional tactics on **MySpace** was for marketers to create **profile pages** for people or fictional characters from their advertising campaigns.
> http://www.nytimes.com/2006/10/16/technology/16social.html?fta=y

> Each "programme" is viewed via its own **profile page** on **Bebo** – and also, in the case of Kate Modern, on **MySpace** and **YouTube**. The idea is to make the content widely available, then draw the audience back to Bebo to interact.
> http://www.guardian.co.uk/media/2007/nov/12/mondaymediasection.technology

As of March 2009, it is still not possible to run a similar search using the entire World Wide Web (including the now-defunct Web pages!) as a linguistic corpus in order to compare the frequencies of the use of *profile page* in the 1990s and the 2000s. Nevertheless, even the results yielded by the Google News Archive Search (that can be seen as a corpus of newspaper texts)—the facts that (1) during the last three years English-speaking journalists used *profile page* six times more often than in the 1990s; as well as that (2) they used it mainly in connection with PROFILES2_2.0—clearly indicate that there exists a much closer conceptual link between the concept of a Web page and that of PROFILE2_2.0 than between the former and PROFILE2_1.0: Whereas PROFILE2_1.0 can only *refer* to a Web page, PROFILE2_2.0 can *mean* it as well.

But why is this so? Why is "Web page" part of the conceptual meaning of PROFILE2_2.0 but not of PROFILE2_1.0? On the one hand, this, as already mentioned, can hardly be attributed to any actual differences between PROFILES2_2.0 and PROFILES2_1.0: Both have a physical location on the Internet which is conventionally referred to as *Web page*. On the other hand, however, this may be due to the fact that PROFILES2_2.0 contain such items as "Blog," "Videos," "Comments from friends," etc., which we usually do not find in PROFILES2_1.0. The point here is this: An SNS profile page containing all these items bears a remarkable (structural and functional) resemblance to a classical homepage/personal Web site. Indeed, both SNS profile pages and traditional homepages seem to be created for essentially the same purpose: to attract the attention of other Internet users (cf. Döring 2002 and references therein). Like SNS profile pages, traditional homepages usually contain at least some description of the person whom they represent (cf. "Official profile page for…" vs. "Official homepage of…"), not to mention the fact that both contain texts, photos, videos, etc. Like SNS profile pages, many traditional homepages have "Guest books," i.e., the place where page visitors can leave public messages. Like SNS profile pages, many traditional homepages have "Friends," i.e., hyperlinks directing to pages of other people/organizations.

In sum, almost everything we know about traditional homepages seems to be true of SNS profiles. Given this and given that homepages had appeared long before SNS profiles, it can be conjectured that the former represents a more familiar concept serving as the source domain for the metaphorical conceptualization of the latter. That SNS PROFILE PAGES ARE HOMEPAGES explains why the former are so often referred to as *pages on the Internet, personal Web sites, homepages*, etc.

As for PROFILES$2\_1.0$, they are almost never referred to in this way because, apart from being located somewhere on the Internet, they are in no other respect similar to homepages. The most important functional difference is that in contrast to homepages and SNS profiles, PROFILES$2\_1.0$ are not supposed to attract the attention of (a large number of) other Internet users. Instead, the majority (if not all) of such profiles are created by Web users who want to stay anonymous when posting in an Internet forum or chatting via IRC. This explains why PROFILES$2\_1.0$ usually (1) contain a rather small amount of user-specific information; (2) abound in empty fields; (3) represent their owners with usernames and avatars instead of users' names and photos, etc. Taking this into account, it must be clear that (1) PROFILES$2\_1.0$ can hardly be analogized to homepages/personal Web sites; as well as that (2) "Web page" can only be the *extension* (not the intension!) of PROFILE$2\_1.0$.

4.4. Origin of the homepage metaphor

The claim that SNS profiles are metaphorized as traditional personal Web sites raises the question of whether SNS creators have always conceptualized the former in terms of the latter. In other words, had the metaphor SNS PROFILE PAGES ARE TRADITIONAL HOMEPAGES been one of the motivations that led to the creation of online social networks? (That is, we will create SNSs to enable Web users to utilize their member profiles in a similar way as classical homepages.)

My answer to this question is no, even though there are several facts suggesting that the answer should be yes. Perhaps the most powerful linguistic argument in favor of the yes-answer is that PROFILES$2\_2.0$ contain such items as "Guest book," "Blog," "Friends," "Videos," etc., which are hardly predictable from either the intension or the extension of *profile*—the word which means "description of someone" and refers to an entity containing such a description, e.g., newspaper article, book, Web page, etc.—but are easily predictable from the extension of *homepage*: homepages, as just mentioned, usually contain at least some of these items. Of course, we can argue that things like "Blog," "Guest book," "Videos," etc., contribute to the overall effect produced by SNS profiles or, in other words, *describe* their owners. This, however, would not account for the fact that these items are so closely associated with PROFILES2_2.0 but are extremely untypical of PROFILES2_1.0. Therefore, instead of searching for an a posteriori explanation of what the word *profile* might have in common with things like "Blog," "Videos," "Guest book," etc., we can hypothesize that the presence of these items on SNS profiles is due to the original (i.e., SNS creators') conceptualization of an SNS profile as a counterpart of a traditional personal Web site. That is, the creators of these services knew that SNS PROFILES WILL BECOME USERS' PERSONAL WEB SITES and therefore decided to integrate some of the homepage-related items (e.g., "Guest books," "Friends," etc.) into SNS profiles. Conversely, PROFILES2_1.0 have never been thought of as an alternative to homepages and therefore do not have "Blog," "Guest book," "Videos," and items alike.

The suggestion that SNS profiles have always been analogized to homepages/personal Web sites can also be backed by the well-known fact that a considerable number of Internet users do not have personal Web sites. As, e.g., Döring (2002) points out, "homepage owners […] constitute a minority of 10% within the Internet population." The reason for this is that creating and maintaining such a presence on the Internet requires the knowledge of HTML—a special markup language in which Web pages are written. In addition to this, Web site owners (usually) have to pay for Web hosting—a service of hosting a client's Web site on a provider's server.

Given these two facts, it can be conjectured that the metaphor SNS PROFILES ARE HOMEPAGES, or, in other words, the idea that SNS profiles could become an alternative to HTML-based traditional homepages could have been one of the motivations triggering the development of SNS profiles which would (1) have the functional potential of HTML-based homepages; but (2) require zero knowledge of HTML on the part of profile owners; and (3) be free, i.e., SNS users would not have to pay to SNS providers for hosting their profile pages. And, as of March 2009, SNS profiles (1) are indeed often used in essentially the same way as traditional personal Web sites (e.g., Hillary Clinton's MySpace profile); (2) can be easily customized (updated, edited, etc.) via an SNS's interface (which, as rule, does not require the knowledge of HTML); and (3) are free of charge.

Nonetheless, despite the seeming plausibility of the arguments above, I insist on the claim that the metaphor SNS PROFILES ARE USERS' PERSONAL WEB SITES had not existed before the emergence of SNSs. The chief reason for this is that according to most SNSs, the focus of these services is on social networking, not on hosting personal Web sites. For example, according to facebook.com, Facebook can be used (1) to keep up with friends and family; (2) share photos and videos; (3) control privacy online; and (4) reconnect with old classmates. MySpace.com describes MySpace as a service for (1) Friends who want to talk online; (2) Single people who want to meet other Singles; (3) Matchmakers who want to connect their friends with other friends; (4) Families who want to keep in touch; (5) Business people and co-workers interested in networking; (6) Classmates and study partners; (7) Anyone looking for long lost friends. According to bebo.com, "Bebo is the next generation social networking service where members can stay in touch with their College friends, connect with friends, share photos, discover new interests and just hang out." However, not a single word is said about an opportunity to launch a personal Web site that could be run by users without the knowledge of HTML.

In addition to this, a number of PROFILE2_2.0-related items can hardly be seen as extra-linguistic realizations of the mapping of the concept of homepage onto an SNS profile. A good example is blog. As mentioned in Chapter 2, blogs are, like SNSs, folksonomies, and wikis, also often described as a hallmark of Web 2.0. As O'Reilly (2005: online) points out, "One of the most highly touted features of the Web 2.0 era is the rise of blogging." (More than that, in O'Reilly's view, blog pages (not SNS profiles!) represent the Web 2.0 alternative to traditional personal Web sites.)

Finally, let us consider "Friends"—the section which we called one of the necessary and sufficient criteria of PROFILE2_2.0-hood. As suggested above, "Friends" of SNS profiles might be "related" with "Friends" of traditional personal Web sites. Thus both the former and the latter stand for essentially the same thing—hyperlinks directing to other Internet pages. The only technical difference is perhaps the fact that in the case of SNS profiles, only a limited number of Internet pages—those which are profile pages of other members of the same SNS—can become "Friends." Traditional personal Web sites, by contrast, allow their owners to list any Web page as a "Friend."

Nonetheless, despite these similarities, it is extremely unlikely that "Friends" of SNS profiles have ever been analogized to "Friends" of traditional personal Web sites. The former plays a far more important role in the structure of an SNS profile than does the latter in the structure of a traditional personal Web site: A profile without "Friends" is not an SNS profile because the concept of a friend is the defining feature of SNS-hood. (For example, MySpace calls itself "a place for friends.") But the same cannot be said about traditional personal Web sites. "Friend" is definitely not a defining feature of homepage-hood/personal Web site-hood: Web sites remain homepages/personal Web sites regardless of the presence/absence of (hyperlinks referred to as) "Friends."

Given these facts, it can be concluded that the homepage metaphor is not the original SNS creators' conception of an SNS profile but the product of the process of re-conceptualization. As is well-known in diachronic semantics, words change their meanings when technology changes the referents which they denote. Consider, for example, the word *car*. As Ullmann (1970) points out,

Our modern cars bear little resemblance to the Celtic wagons of the first century B.C.; yet the technological development was so continuous that there was no need for the label to be replaced at any point, and the word has remained phonetically almost unaltered since Roman times. (p. 199)

Similar to the word *car* which originally referred to a primitive four-wheeled Celtic wagon but now stands for an automobile, the word *profile* originally (i.e., in the Web 1.0 era) referred to a Web page containing a short description of a user who wanted to stay anonymous when posting in an Internet forum or chatting via IRC, but nowadays can also stand for a Web site which is utilized in a variety of ways: e.g., for communicating with friends, publishing blog entries, uploading videos, etc. However, in addition to the fact that *profile* came to have a different extension, its intension changed as well: As a result of the technological development described above, the concept signified by *profile*—the intensional meaning "information about a user"—could no longer remain the motivating link mediating between the word *profile* and its new referent—a Web site where users communicate with friends, post blog entries, upload videos, etc. As a result of this, SNS users were confronted with the necessity to fill out the conceptual gap, i.e., to find a new concept that would keep the two things—the word *profile* and its new referent—together. And they solved the task by analogizing SNS profiles to things well-known to them since the early years of the Internet—classical homepages/traditional personal Web sites which perform the same function as SNS profiles.

To conclude: It was users who re-conceptualized SNS profiles as homepages/traditional personal Web sites. The reason for this, however, was that the creators enabled them to use the former in essentially the same way as the latter, i.e., to have almost the same amount of power over their profile pages as owners of traditional personal Web sites have over their homepages, e.g., be able to (1) easily customize their profiles; (2) upload music, photos, and videos; (3) publish texts in the form of blog entries; (4) receive feedback from profile visitors through guest books; etc. The reason for this was that the creators wanted to attract the maximum number of users to their services through (1) multi-functionality of member profiles (i.e., an SNS profile is not only a description of the profile owner but her/his publishing space for blog entries, photos, and videos, and so on); as well as (2) their easy customizability.

The claim that the homepage metaphor emerged as a result of the re-conceptualization of SNS profiles through users is based on empirical evidence (which will be discussed below) suggesting that it is users (and not creators) who conceptualize SNS profiles as homepages and SNS services as Web hosting services. However, it is important to note that there is absolutely nothing which would a priori disqualify creators from being the locus of such re-conceptualization. For everything that was said above—the necessity to fill out the conceptual gap—equally applies to both sides: users and creators. Nonetheless, it was users who metaphorized SNS profiles as homepages and SNS services as Web hosting services. The main empirical evidence for this is that (1) with the exception of myFriendsReunited.com, not a single SNS explicitly refers to its profiles as homepages/personal Web sites; and (2) none of the SNSs describes itself as a Web hosting service. In contrast, users often refer to profiles as *homepages* and SNS services as *Web hosting services*. For example, MySpace and Facebook are often analogized to GeoCities, a popular free Web site provider that was founded in 1994. As, e.g., Mark Keitges points out,

> The first thing that comes to mind when looking at the average MySpace profile is the early days of Geocities and other free Web site providers. Users would create very ugly Web sites containing jarring backgrounds, photos placed everywhere without any mind for proximity and likely have an annoying song playing in the background.
> http://www.yankton.net/stories/021508/riv_247219729.shtml

In a similar way, the blogger Zach argues that

> MySpace is the new Geocities. Home to everyone who THINKS they have a "homepage". Mostly kids who sit at home and add atrocious backgrounds and annoying animated gif's.
> http://tinyurl.com/dnjflv

Likewise, an anonymous blogger laments that

> Myspace is the 2003 version of Geocities. The personal pages are just as hack, the communications are just as shallow, a 'place for friends' is a misnomer.
> http://www.in8sworld.net/blog/archives/462

The idea that SNS PROFILES OF 2004-2009 ARE HOMEPAGES OF THE MID 1990s was also articulated in a recent World Street Journal article by Dennis K. Berman:

> Facebook founder Mark Zuckerberg was 10 years old when David Bohnett, then a 37-year-old mainframe programmer, hatched an idea: Set up a Web-based "community" where young people could divulge their most intimate feelings. He grouped those musings into different themes, and ushered in advertisers to hawk Volvos and Volkswagens. ***This ur-Facebook of 1994 was called GeoCities*** [...]
> ***Back then, entries were known as home pages, not profiles***. But the basic, expressive elements of today's Facebook and competitor MySpace, owned by News Corp., were all right there. (Wall Street Journal, 25.09.2007, my emphasis)
> http://www.bohnettfoundation.org/news_stories/view/100741

And there are many other blog entries, Web forum comments, and newspaper articles claiming that services like Facebook and MySpace only insignificantly differ from Web hosting services like GeoCities which have been online since the mid 1990s.

As for the creators' perspective—i.e., the question of why they are reluctant to admit that SOCIAL NETWORKING SERVICES ARE WEB HOSTING SERVICES—the following explanation seems plausible: Contrary to Web hosting services which have been well-known since the early years of the Internet, SNS services, as often contended, represent a relatively new phenomenon that has only recently become part of our mainstream culture (see boyd and Ellison 2007). Accordingly, for SNS creators it is far more advantageous to call their services *social networking services* (thereby implying that they have created something new, something original, something that has not previously existed on the Internet) instead of *Web hosting services*.

5. Friend

In this chapter, we will deal with "Friends"—one of the necessary and sufficient criteria of PROFILE2_2.0-hood and the defining concept of SNS-hood. As usual, let us begin with the referential meaning of the lexeme under consideration.

5.1. Extension

As mentioned in the previous chapter, "Friends" of SNS profiles are hyperlinks directing to profile pages of other members of the same SNS (see screenshot 5). However, it is extremely unlikely that SNS users have hyperlinks in mind when talking about their SNS friends. Thus, as correctly pointed out by Woiskunski (2001: 310-311), one of the hallmarks of the global computer network is that people are present there not in their entirety but by means of texts, photos and videos, etc., which they post on their personal Web sites, blog or profile pages, job seekers databases, Web forums, guest books, etc. This "reduction" of people on the Internet gives rise to the metonymy PEOPLE FOR WHAT THEY POST ON THE INTERNET.

Consider, for example, the sentence *MySpace is an online community that lets you meet your friends' friends* from the MySpace "About Us" page.[1] Given the PEOPLE FOR WHAT THEY POST ON THE INTERNET metonymy, it must be clear that this statement cannot be true: It is impossible to meet anybody on MySpace or on any other similar Internet service. The only thing that can be "met" there are member profiles (consisting of texts, photos and videos, etc.) maintained by members of these services.

However, as just said, it is extremely unlikely that non-linguists are aware of the fact that *friends* in *meet your friends' friends* does not really refer to users but to their member profiles. The reason for this is that the metonymy PEOPLE FOR WHAT THEY POST ON THE INTERNET is a default metonymy. That is, a metonymy which is not consciously recognized as a metonymy because, in it, the choice of the vehicle concept fulfills at least some of the maxims of the principle of cognitive salience such as, for example, HUMAN OVER NON-HUMAN, CONCRETE OVER ABSTRACT, INTERACTIONAL OVER NON-INTERACTIONAL, IMMEDIATE OVER NON-IMMEDIATE, DOMINANT OVER LESS DOMINANT, GOOD GESTALT OVER POOR GESTALT, CENTRAL OVER PERIPHERAL, IMPORTANT OVER LESS IMPORTANT, etc. As argued by Kövecses and Radden (1998),

> the more of [these] principles apply to a particular metonymic expression, the greater the cognitive motivation. As a result, the metonymy will be regarded as natural or "default". (p. 71)

---

[1] http://www.myspace.com/index.cfm?fuseaction=misc.aboutus

For example, the sentence *let's go to the theatre* which does not mean "let's move to the building of a particular theatre" (which it literally stands for) but "let's watch a play" seems to fulfill at least two of these maxims: (1) INTERACTIONAL OVER NON-INTERACTIONAL: we interact with theatres (i.e., go to their buildings, buy tickets, watch plays, etc.), but not with plays which we only watch there; and (2) IMMEDIATE OVER NON-IMMEDIATE: we, first of all, go to the building of a theatre and only then watch a play. Similarly, the vehicle concept FRIENDS in *meet your friends' friends* fulfills the maxims (1) HUMAN OVER NON-HUMAN: friends are human; their member profiles are non-human; (2) INTERACTIONAL OVER NON-INTERACTIONAL: SNS users interact with other users, not with their member profiles; (3) DOMINANT OVER LESS DOMINANT: SNS users are profile owners and thus have the absolute power over them (i.e., can change them anytime they want); and (4) IMPORTANT OVER LESS IMPORTANT: For SNS users, it is much more important to find their friends in their entirety (and in this way be able to interact with them) rather than their member profiles only.

Given these facts, we can conclude that the intended referential meaning of *friends* is, of course, neither "hyperlinks directing to profile pages of other members of the same SNS" nor "profile pages themselves" (consisting of texts produced by these people). *Friend*, as understood by both SNS users and creators, stands for a particular user of the same SNS—the one whose name can be found in the profile's "Friends" section; the one who was "added as a friend."

5.2. Intension

5.2.1. SNS friends versus traditional friends

Having established what *friend* stands for, let us now proceed to its intensional semantics. The most interesting issue here is the relationship between an SNS friend (FRIEND2) and the traditional concept of friend(ship) (FRIEND1) associated with the signifier *friend*: "one that seeks the society or welfare of another whom he holds in affection, respect, or esteem or whose companionship and personality are pleasurable" (Merriam-Webster Unabridged), "a person you know well and regard with affection and trust" (WordNet), "a person whom one knows, likes, and trusts" (American Heritage Dictionary), "one joined to another in mutual benevolence and intimacy" (Oxford English Dictionary), etc. Does FRIEND2 mean the same thing as FRIEND1? If not, what is then the intensional meaning of FRIEND2?

As far as the first question is concerned, it is quite obvious that the answer can only be no: In the overwhelming majority of cases, FRIEND2 cannot be equated with FRIEND1 (even though it is possible that some SNS members are using these services for communicating with their real-life friends, so that

FRIEND2 = FRIEND1). First of all, it must be noted that SNS users usually have much more FRIENDS2 than they have FRIENDS1. Thus, as reported by the blogger Elias Bizannes,[2] among 1000 Facebook users who took part in the poll "How many friends do you have on Facebook?" (which was conducted in July 2007), 559 said that they had between 100 and 400 FRIENDS2. Likewise, in a recent study by Ellison et al. (2007: 1153), it is reported that the average Facebook user has between 150-200 FRIENDS2 listed in her/his profile's "Friends" section.

That 100-400 FRIENDS2 which Facebook users have in their member profiles cannot be FRIENDS1 follows from the fact that it is physically impossible to communicate with so many people on a regular basis, as Elias Bizannes correctly points out. (And as Kövecses (1995: 320) points out, communication is perhaps the most prominent property of friendship in Western cultures.) Thus, in a recent article *Social Network Size in Humans*, the British sociologists Russell Hill and Robert Dunbar (2003: 53) argue that in contemporary Western societies, the "maximum network size average[s] 153.5 individuals, with a mean network size of 124.9 for those individuals explicitly contacted." To put it in a simpler way: Our entire social networks—i.e., all people we communicate with including our friends, relatives, work colleagues, etc.—rarely consist of more than 154 people.

As for the number of FRIENDS1, consider the following quote from the same article:

> Previous studies have suggested that social networks may be hierarchically differentiated, with larger numbers of progressively less intense relationships maintained at higher levels. Dunbar (1998) suggested that clusterings of relationships tended to occur at 5 (support cliques), 12–15 (sympathy groups), and 35 (bands) individuals, with further higher-level groupings at 500 and 1500–2000 (equating in the ethnographic literature to mega-bands and tribes, respectively). Support cliques (defined as all those individuals from whom one would seek advice, support, or help in times of severe emotional or financial distress) averaged 4.72 (±2.95) individuals in one UK sample (Dunbar and Spoor 1995) and 3.01 (±1.77) in a US sample (Marsden 1987) [...] (p. 67)

In other words, among 154 members of our social networks, no more than five are likely to qualify as our (close/best) friends, i.e., people "from whom [we] would seek advice, support, or help in times of severe emotional or financial distress."

It is not quite clear whether the same can be said about sympathy groups. According to Buys and Larson (1979; discussed in ibid. p. 67), members of this group are "individuals whose death would be personally devastating." The point here is that apart from relatives and friends, we can also be devastated by the

---

[2] http://liako.biz/2007/07/facebook-poll-how-many-friends-do-you-have/

death of a classmate or a work colleague—i.e., people whom we do not necessarily consider our friends. Anyway, even if we add 15 members of a sympathy group to five members of a support clique, we still have only 20 people who could be referred to as our *friends* in the traditional meaning of this word.

The claim that FRIEND2 ≠ FRIEND1 can also be given credence by the existence of the "Best Friend" application that allows Facebook users to assign their friends to a particular category: "Best Friend," Boyfriend/Girlfriend," "Husband/Wife," Father/Mother," etc. Likewise, on hi5, users can distinguish between "Friends" and "Top Friends" or, alternatively, like on Facebook, assign them to a particular category (called *friend circle*): "College," "Classmates," "Work Buddies," "Close Friends," etc. Given these applications, it can be concluded that FRIEND2 has a broader meaning than FRIEND1: It appears that FRIENDS2 can include not only FRIENDS1 but also any other member of a user's social network such as relatives, classmates, work buddies, etc. If this were not the case, SNS providers would never think of giving their users an opportunity to distinguish between "Friends" and "Top Friends" or assign "Friends" to categories like "Buddies," "Classmates," "Girlfriend/Boyfriend," etc.

Finally, it must be observed that the question "What is a friend on an SNS like MySpace or Facebook?" has been "traversing the blogosphere," as the blogger Ethan Demme[3] points out. Indeed, if you search the Web for, e.g., "How many friends do you have?" or "What is a friend?", you will find a number of blog entries and Web forum comments devoted to the comparison of the meanings of FRIEND2 and FRIEND1.

As an illustration of this, consider the remark of the user Charlie about the loss of the distinction between a friend and an acquaintance:

> I think the distinction between a friend and an acquaintance is really lost on Facebook. Most of my close friends aren't on Facebook and yet I've still managed to accumulate over 80 'friends'. Some of these 'friends' I have only met a couple of times. Some I haven't seen for over 15 years.
> http://liako.biz/2007/07/facebook-poll-how-many-friends-do-you-have/

In contrast to Charlie, the blogger Steve Rubel does not attempt to analogize FRIEND2 to an acquaintance or any other similar concept but subscribes to the view that SNSs have changed the traditional concept of friendship:

> It seems, at least to me, that how we define who is/isn't a friend has changed dramatically [...] Some people I know [...] like to regularly brag about how many friends they have on Facebook. I don't blame them for saying so. I blame society. In America at least, he/she who can dies with the most friends – even if they are virtual – "wins."
> It's clear from all of this that our entire concept of friendship [...] is changing. It's becoming more about quantity and less about quality. [...]

---

[3] http://ethandemme.com/blog/?p=67

> It leaves me all confused about what friendship will look like in 10 years. It seems like it's declining in quality, even as technology scales it in quantity and helps our networks spread far and wide.
> http://www.micropersuasion.com/2007/08/how-the-web-cha.html

The idea that friendship is nowadays "declining in quality" is also expressed in a recent Telegraph article by Roger Highfield and Nic Fleming who point out that

> Some people can be designated "friends," without having to reciprocate. [These] are "trophy friends" [...]
> There is even software – notably MySpace Whore and MySpace Whore Train – "which automates part of the friendship procedure." This can allow people to "collect friends like boys collect Airfix models." (Telegraph, 10.09.2007)
> http://tinyurl.com/de22o3

To conclude: FRIEND2 cannot have the same intensional meaning as FRIEND1. The reasons for this include (1) the physical impossibility of having so many FRIENDS1; (2) the existence of "Best Friend" and other similar applications allowing SNS users to either distinguish between "Friends" and "Top friends" or classify FRIENDS2 into categories like "Buddies," "Classmates," "Close friends," etc.; and (3) the popularity of this topic in the blogosphere, which suggests that many users are consciously aware of the fact that FRIEND2 ≠ FRIEND1. Proceeding from these observations, let us now try to answer the most important question of this chapter: What is the intensional meaning of FRIEND2?

As stated earlier, it appears that the lexeme FRIEND2 has a broader meaning than FRIEND1: Whereas the latter can only refer to members of an individual's support clique (and perhaps also sympathy groups), the former can stand for any member of a user's social network. As suggested by the Facebook user Charlie, FRIEND2 means "acquaintance," i.e., "a person whom one knows" (American Heritage Dictionary), "persons with whom one is acquainted" (Merriam-Webster Unabridged), etc.

Empirically, this suggestion can be supported by the fact that the concept of an acquaintance had been one of the senses of *friend* before the rise of SNSs. Thus, according to the 2000 edition of the American Heritage Dictionary, *friend* does not only mean FRIEND1 (i.e., a person whom one knows, likes, and trusts"), but also "a person whom one knows; an acquaintance." So, it turns out that people like Steve Rubel who lament that friendship is nowadays declining in quality and even blame the society for this fail to understand a very simple fact: The word *friend* is polysemous and, in the SNS context, signifies "acquaintance," not "FRIEND1."

However, if FRIEND2 does indeed mean "acquaintance," there cannot but arise the question of why the creators of so many (if not all) SNSs have decided in favor of the signifier *friend* which is still much closer associated with the traditional concept of friendship than with that of acquaintanceship. Why couldn't they use the word *acquaintance* itself? Or perhaps *contacts*?

Contacts is the term which performs the same function on ICQ (Skype, and many other) interfaces as *friends* does on SNS profiles. Similar to SNS users who are added as *friends*, ICQ users are added as *contacts*. Similar to SNS friends who can be classified into categories like "Buddies," "Close friends," "Classmates," etc., ICQ contacts can be classified into groups like "Family," "Friends," "Co-workers," etc.

There is no doubt that *contacts* would verbalize the concept of FRIEND2 in a much better way than *friends*: *Contacts* does not specify the degree of relationship between the user and her/his contacts and is therefore much less controversial than *friend* which, as stated previously, is still strongly associated with its central meaning "a person whom one knows, likes, and trusts." If *friends* were *contacts*, Steve Rubel would perhaps not argue that friendship is nowadays declining in quality. So the question here is: Why did SNS creators choose the word *friend*?

5.2.2. Why *friend*?

To answer this question, let us, first of all, consider the etymology of *friend*. According to the American Heritage Dictionary:

> A friend is a lover, literally. The relationship between Latin *amicus* "friend" and *amo* "I love" is clear, as is the relationship between Greek *philos* "friend" and *phileo* "I love." In English, though, we have to go back a millennium before we see the verb related to *friend*. At that time, *freond*, the Old English word for "friend," was simply the present participle of the verb *freon*, "to love." The Germanic root behind this verb is *fri*, which meant "to like, love, be friendly to."
> http://www.bartleby.com/61/71/F0327100.html

Particularly interesting here is not that *friend* originally meant "lover" but the direction of semantic change: "lover" > "friend" > "acquaintance." The point here is that at each stage the word *friend* came to signify a less important interpersonal relationship: love > friendship > mere acquaintance with somebody. This leads us to the following question: What is the reason for using *lover* to refer to somebody who is not a lover but a friend? (For the word *friend* which originally meant "lover" could acquire the meaning "friend" only because at some point language users started to use the word *friend* to refer to people who were not lovers but friends.) And what is the reason for using *friend* to refer to somebody who is not a friend but an acquaintance?

One possible answer to this question is politeness. As is well-known in linguistics, politeness is one of the central principles of human communication. Similar to the cooperative principle of Herbert Paul Grice, politeness or the principle of polite behavior (formulated by Geoffrey Leech) consists of a set of maxims explaining what it means to be polite when communicating with other people. Consider, for example, the maxim of praise: Minimize dispraise of the hearer/Maximize praise of the hearer (Cruse 2004: 37). What this means is that in order to be polite, we have to say things pleasing the hearer's ears. For example, we say *Thank you so much for inviting me. I had an absolutely wonderful time!* even if we were actually bored to death. The consequence of this is that trying to fulfill the maxim of praise, language users are constantly changing the referential meaning of a great number of expressions: We say *wonderful time* to refer to a bad time, even though *wonderful* does not really mean "bad" but the opposite of it. And this, as is well-known, often leads to semantic change, i.e., at some point we accept that *wonderful* no longer means "wonderful" but "bad." (Or that "bad" is one of the meanings of *wonderful*.)

As an illustration of this, consider the German word *Frau* "woman" which goes back to the Middle High German *vrouwe* "lady"—the term which in Medieval times was associated with the concept of courtly love. The fact that the word *lady* acquired the meaning "woman" is often attributed to politeness (Keller and Kirschbaum 2003: 12): That is, German men, trying to maximize praise of their beloved women, started to use the word *vrouwe* "lady" to refer to women who, strictly speaking, did not "deserve" to be referred in this way (because the term *vrouwe* was reserved for female nobility, whereas all other women were called *wip*), so that at some point *vrouwe* "lady" was re-conceptualized as "woman."

Taking this into account, we can hypothesize that *friend*—the word which originally meant "lover/beloved"—came to mean "friend" because our ancestors, trying to maximize praise of their friends, started to call them *lovers/beloveds*. (By the way, consider the phrase *beloved friend* which is still in use today.) In a similar way, we can argue that *friend* came to mean "acquaintance" because we, trying to maximize praise of our acquaintances, started to call them *friends*. (A good illustration of this is the extremely "insincere" use of *friend* by politicians, e.g., by Western leaders describing their Russian counterparts: *My friend Mikhail Gorbachev* (Margaret Thatcher), *My friend Boris Yeltsin* (Bill Clinton), *My friend Vladimir Putin* (George Bush, Jr.).) And finally, we can suggest that SNS creators decided in favor of the signifier *friends* (not *acquaintances* or *contacts*) in order to maximize praise of users of these services who, as stated earlier, cannot have 100-400 FRIENDS[1]. Indeed, the fact that SNS users have so many "friends" in their profiles' "Friends" sections cannot but please their ears. It flatters them. It is supposed to produce an impression that they are successful people interesting for many other people. This is the reason why some users "like to regularly brag about how many friends they have on Facebook." This is one of the reasons why some users are even ready to resort to friend adders, i.e., software allowing them to automatically add other users as friends; sometimes even in such a way that "friended" users do not have an opportunity to decline a friend request.

In addition to politeness, the choice of the signifier *friends* can also be explained using prototype theory (PT) (see, e.g., Lakoff 1987). As stated earlier, social networks are hierarchically differentiated, i.e., consist of groups such as support cliques, sympathy groups, bands, etc. (Hill and Dunbar 2003: 67). There is no doubt that among these groups, it is support cliques (i.e., our close friends and relatives) which we perceive as the most important part of our social networks. From the PT point of view, this means that friends and relatives are the prototypical representatives of the conceptual category SOCIAL NETWORK. And as is well-known from studies on prototype effects, prototypes serve as categories' reference points. That is, usually the name of a category is used to refer to its prototype. For example, *bird* in *Look, there's a bird on the window sill* will most likely refer to a robin or a dove—birds which, in our culture, are considered better representatives of the category BIRD than, say, peacocks or penguins (Löbner 2002: 176). (However, if it turns out that the bird on the window sill is a penguin (or any other less prototypical bird), we will most likely say *Look, there's a penguin (peacock, ostrich, pheasant, etc.) on the window sill.*) Likewise, the term *social network* usually refers to relatives and friends—best representatives of the conceptual category SOCIAL NETWORK serving as its cognitive reference points.

Consider, for example, the following quotes:

> Many clients falsely assume that an **extensive social network, involving family, friends and colleagues**, just happens. This is blatantly untrue. The maintenance of friendships and relationships requires a certain amount of deliberate effort and hard work: they have to be developed and cultivated. (British National Corpus)

> CONSULTING OTHERS One expectation of the ASW is that others in the patient's **social network --; relatives, friends, neighbours** and so on --; should be consulted to help build a picture of the individual and their behaviour. (British National Corpus)

In both examples, "relatives/family" and "friends" are chosen as an illustration of what the term *social network* stands for. The reason for this is that "friends" and "relatives" represent the prototypical members of the category SOCIAL NETWORK. (By the way, here we observe the prototype effect "order of mention": Members that are considered more prototypical—"relatives" and "friends"—are mentioned earlier than less prototypical "colleagues" and "neighbors." We would be surprised to see "colleagues" and "neighbors" before "friends" and "family.")

Proceeding from these observations, we can now propose the second explanation for the SNS creators' choice of the signifier *friends*. This word was chosen because it stands for one of the best representatives of the conceptual category SOCIAL NETWORK: FRIENDS1. (It is clear that neither *family* nor *relatives* could have been chosen instead of *friends* because the latter has a broader meaning than the former: Relatives/family can be referred to as *friends* (e.g., *my mother is my best friend*), but friends which are not relatives/family cannot be referred as *relatives/family*.)

Before proceeding to the users' perspective, I would like to stress that the two explanations proposed above—the maxim of praise of the pragmatic principle of polite behavior and the prototype effect NAME OF A CATEGORY FOR PROTOTYPE OF THAT CATEGORY—should not be seen as two competing accounts of the same phenomenon. There is no contradiction in arguing that SNS creators chose *friends* because (1) they wanted to maximize praise of SNS users who cannot have so many FRIENDS1; as well as that (2) FRIEND1 is the prototype and thus the reference point of the conceptual category SOCIAL NETWORK. The latter explains why SNS creators chose *friend* instead of any other member of a social network. The former—why they chose *friends* instead of *acquaintances*, *contacts*, or any other similar expression that could be used to refer to any member of a user's social network.

5.2.3. Users

Finally, let us turn to the perspective of SNS users who "friend" people who are not their real-life friends. How did the user Charlie manage to accumulate over 80 FRIENDS2, even though he is aware that these people are not FRIENDS1? Why did all these people ask the user Charlie to add them as his friends? For if they do not qualify as FRIENDS1 for Charlie, it is very likely that Charlie does not qualify as FRIEND1 for them as well.

The answers to these questions are again PT and politeness. As for the former, the user Charlie knows that traditional social networks are structured around FRIENDS1—one of the best representatives of the conceptual category SOCIAL NETWORK. In addition to this, however, he also knows that social networks do not consist of FRIENDS1 only but of all acquaintances: FRIENDS1, work colleagues, classmates, neighbors, etc. This knowledge leads Charlie to the following conclusion: The word *friend*, when used in the context of an SNS profile, is the metonym for *social network*—that is, the term that denotes any member of a user's social network. Accordingly, when Charlie receives a friend request from somebody who is not FRIEND1 but an acquaintance, he does not decline it because the person who sent the request is not FRIEND1. Instead, Charlie accepts her/him as his "friend" (i.e., as FRIEND2) because FRIEND2, as understood by Charlie, does not mean "FRIEND1," but "acquaintance." This explains why Charlie has managed to accumulate so many FRIENDS2, even though most of his close friends are still not on Facebook. Indeed, as he points out, "some of these 'friends' I have only met a couple of times. Some I haven't seen for over 15 years." (And the same can be said about Charlie's Facebook friends who requested Charlie to add them as his friends, even though they do not think of Charlie as FRIEND1. They did so because they consider Charlie an acquaintance, a member of their social networks.)

At the same time, however, it is obvious that politeness plays here an extremely important role as well. By accepting a friend request from somebody who is not a friend but an acquaintance, Charlie avoids a face-threatening act (FTA). As argued by Goffman (1956; discussed in Renkema 2004: 25), "every participant in the social process has the need to be appreciated by others and the need to be free and not interfered with." The former is known as *positive face*; the latter as *negative face*. There is no doubt that declining a friend request is an FTA posing a threat to the requester's positive face (i.e., the need to be appreciated). Given this fact, we can hypothesize that most SNS users would try to avoid the FTA when dealing with requests sent by non-friends: As Cory Doctorow argues in a recent InformationWeek article, "It's socially awkward to refuse to add someone to your friends list,"[4] especially if that person is your real-life acquaintance.

However, despite the seeming plausibility of what is said above, neither politeness nor PT can account for the phenomenon of FRIENDS2 who are not users' real-life acquaintances. The point here is that our previous discussion was based on the assumption that FRIEND2 signifies "acquaintance" and is therefore used as the metonym for any member of a user's offline social network. The problem with this account is that under this view, all "friended" users are supposed to be profile owners' real-life acquaintances. However, if turns out that this is not true of at least some of them (i.e., if some of the "friended" users are not members of profile owners' real-life social networks), we can no longer assert that FRIENDS2 = OFFLINE ACQUAINTANCES.

Besides, if ONLINE SOCIAL NETWORKS = OFFLINE SOCIAL NETWORKS, we would have to admit that the claim that SNS PROFILES ARE USERS' PERSONAL WEB SITES is not true. Indeed, if FRIENDS2 = OFFLINE ACQUAINTANCES, it is most likely that SNS member profiles are then conceptualized not as homepages/personal Web sites but as a Web 2.0 alternative to e-mail—a service which can and, as a matter of fact, is actually used for essentially the same purpose: communicating with real-life acquaintances.

In connection with these suggestions, the following comments are called for. First of all, the claims that (1) FRIENDS2 = OFFLINE ACQUAINTANCES; and (2) SOCIAL NETWORKING SERVICES ARE E-MAIL SERVICES do, of course, apply to a presumably very large number of SNS users. For example, as argued by the blogger Ethan Demme, "there are the people who use facebook like it was designed to be used, i.e. just to keep in contact with their friends." However, as the

---

[4] http://tinyurl.com/32vpqe

following remark makes clear, *friends*—as understood by Ethan Demme—are all real-life acquaintances:

> Here is what i've come up with as my mantra for deciding if you are "friend worthy"
> **How do I know thee?**
> Real life friends, relatives, classmates (that I've had a real live conversation with) all these are automatically "friended".
> http://ethandemme.com/2007/08/27/are-you-friend-worthy-on-facebook/

Likewise, the user Hubert states that he adds only those people whom he knows in the real-world:

> I'm 27 and I have 121 friends on Facebook. [...]
> Personally, I only add people that I actually know in real life, that I would say hello to if I met them on the street.
> http://www.allfacebook.com/2007/12/how-many-friends-is-too-many/

As for the suggestion that SOCIAL NETWORKING SERVICES ARE E-MAIL SERVICES, consider the following remark of the blogger Aidan Henry:

> Many of my friends and colleagues are now using the internal Facebook messaging system more than e-mail. It has almost become an e-mail substitute. Having said that, they still check their e-mail as it is essential to daily life on the Internet. Nonetheless, messaging between Facebook members is usually accomplished within the social network rather than e-mail.
> http://www.mappingtheweb.com/2007/07/11/facebook-email/

However, despite these facts, we cannot deny that a considerable number of FRIENDS2 are not real-life acquaintances of those SNS users who added them as friends. Consider, for example, Friendster users' answers to the questions "How many friends do you have on Friendster and "How many of them do you actually know?" from http://tinyurl.com/ctz8of: The user HiLyNkawAii has 824 FRIENDS2 on Friendster but knows only 1/3 of her/his friendslist population. DeverKerbill has 175 FRIENDS2 but knows only one of them. The user babyzchen claims that s/he knows each of her/his 886 FRIENDS2. However, this claim is followed by a smiley. And so on.

Given this, let us now proceed to the most difficult question of this chapter: What is the intensional meaning of FRIEND2 for those SNS users who "friend" people whom they do not know in the real world?

My answer to this question is that in the SNS context, *friend* has come to mean "subscriber to the content generated by the profile owner." To prove this, let us have a look at "Friend subscriptions" on MySpace and "Friend updates" on hi5:

Screenshot 6. "Friend Subscriptions" section on MySpace

Screenshot 7. "Friend Updates" section on hi5

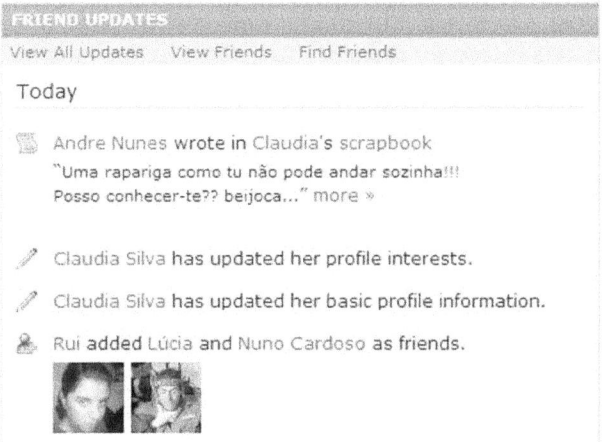

As you can see, both inform the profile owner about the recent activities of her/his FRIENDS2, e.g., whether they posted new blog entries, uploaded new photos and videos, changed their profile information, etc.

The fact that FRIENDS2 ARE SUBSCRIBERS is, undeniably, the most important motivation for "friending" people who are not real-life acquaintances. Indeed, if an SNS user conceptualizes her/his member profile not only as an alternative to e-mail but also as an alternative to traditional homepages/personal Web sites and, as a consequence of this, uses it not only for keeping in touch with her/his real-life acquaintances but also for generating new content such as blog entries, photos and videos, etc., s/he cannot be uninterested in "friending" the maximum number of users, since "Friend Subscriptions" and "Friend Updates" offer a unique opportunity to effectively distribute that content: As soon as s/he uploads a new video or publishes a new blog post, each of her/his FRIENDS2 will be automatically notified about this by means of the "Subscription" section.

That FRIENDS2 ARE SUBSCRIBERS is almost always true of celebrity profiles. For example, on March 2, 2009 Hillary Clinton's MySpace profile listed 165887 MySpace users as her friends. It is obvious that the overwhelming majority of these people are not Hillary Clinton's real-life acquaintances but Internet users from around the globe most of whom were "friended" during Hillary Clinton's 2008 presidential campaign when her profile was actively used as a publishing space for blog entries, videos, new clips, and items alike. Accordingly, these "friends" were conceptualized by Hillary Clinton/people responsible for maintaining her MySpace profile as subscribers to this content. Likewise, users who added Hillary Clinton as their FRIEND2 did so because they wanted to subscribe to her profile, i.e., be regularly notified about the availability of new items of content on her profile.

That FRIENDS2 ARE SUBSCRIBERS also explains why some SNS users resort to friend adders. Consider, for example, the below description of FriendFrost:

> Make thousands of friends with our myspace friend adder
> Welcome to FriendFrost!
> FriendFrost is a free myspace friend adder. We help you promote your band, business, website, or just to receive THOUSANDS of friends with our free myspace adder.
> http://friendfrost.com/

Given this description, it is clear that the main motivation for using friend adders is self-promotion or, being more exact, promotion of the content which profile owners post on their profile pages. The more FRIENDS2 (i.e., subscribers) they have in their friends lists, the more people will learn about new blog entries, photos and videos, music, etc., published on their profiles.

5.3. Social networks and traditional concept of friendship

At the end of this chapter, let us briefly return to Steve Rubel's claim that SNSs have changed the traditional concept of friendship. Given the findings of the previous sections, we can conclude that this is not so. Social networks did expand the word *friend* with two new meanings: "any member of a user's social network" and "subscriber to the content generated by the profile owner." But the traditional concept of friendship has remained the same. A "traditional" friend is still a "person whom we know well and regard with affection and trust," as defined by, e.g., WordNet.

As for the future of friendship, consider the following quote from a recent non-linguistic article devoted to SNSs:

> [I]n the context of SNS moving into the cultural mainstream, the 'everyday sense' of friend can often be the SNS Friend. So what we are missing here is a sense of the recursive nature of these processes as SNS become mundane and as the version of friendship they offer be-

gins to remediate and shape understandings of friendship more generally. [...] We can imagine this as a recursive process where SNS come to challenge and possibly even mutate understandings of friendship. It is conceivable [...] that understandings and values of friendship may be altered by engagements with SNS. (Beer 2008: 520)

I disagree with this assessment. First of all, because there is no such thing as an SNS Friend: An SNS Friend, as we have established in this chapter, can be (1) FRIEND1; (2) any other member of a user's offline social network (e.g., parent, former classmate, etc.); and (3) a subscriber to the content generated by the profile owner. Accordingly, the so-called "everyday day" sense of *friend* can be the SNS Friend only when an SNS Friend = FRIEND1 or a real-life acquaintance. However, when an SNS Friend = subscriber, the everyday sense of *friend* cannot be the SNS Friend, for it is only the SNS context where users can subscribe to other users' profiles. Accordingly, the idea that "understandings and values of friendship may be altered by engagements with SNS" can only be true of the "subscriber" sense of *friend*. But has the "subscriber" sense affected the "friend" sense? Will the "subscriber" sense replace the traditional concept of friendship? As far as the first question is concerned, the answer is again no. As stated earlier, the "friend" sense still exists. Not only in real-life but also on SNSs where it is often verbalized by the expressions *close friend/best friend* (e.g., in the context of the "Best friend" application on Facebook and similar applications on other SNSs). As for the second question, it is theoretically possible that *friend* will no longer mean "FRIEND1" but "subscriber." However, in this case, the concept of FRIEND1 will have to be verbalized by another lexeme such as, e.g., *acquaintance*.

6. Pokes, fives, smiles...

The last chapter of this part will be devoted to "poking"—a way of contacting an SNS user characteristic of Facebook, hi5, Friendster, and some other SNSs which can be seen as an alternative to friend requests and e-mail-like private messages (PMs). From the referential point of view, the essence of poking is as follows. When user A "pokes" user B, the SNS, which both A and B are members of, sends user B a notification that s/he was "poked" by user A.

According to facebook.com,

> The poke feature can be used for a variety of things on Facebook. For instance, you can poke your friends to say hello. If you poke a user who normally does not have access to your profile, they will be able to temporarily see your Basic Info, Work Info, and Education Info. When you poke someone, they will receive a poke alert on their home page. http://www.facebook.com/help/question.php?id=124498

As just said, Facebook is not the only SNS platform where users can communicate in such an interesting way. However, in contrast to *friend* which on all SNSs serves as the metonym for *social network*, the POKING concept is verbalized by multiple signifiers. For example, if you are a member of hi5, you *give fives*. If you have an account on Friendster, you *send smiles*. On StudiVZ, users *gruddle* (i.e., greet and cuddle) each other.

As in the case of *friend*, the most interesting issue here is the conceptual meaning of these expressions. Does *poke*, for example, really mean "hello," given that Facebook users "poke their friends to say hello"? Does the traditional concept of poking influence how Internet users poke each other on Facebook? For example, is it polite to poke a stranger in the context of an online SNS, given that it is not polite to do so in real-life?

As with *friend* and *profile*, we will approach these questions from the perspective of (1) the creators of Facebook, hi5, and Friendster who integrated pokes, fives, and smiles into their services; as well as of (2) these SNSs' users who use these features *for a variety of things* such as, e.g., *saying hello to other users*.

6.1. Creators

As a first approximation, it can be observed that all these expressions qualify as referential metaphors since all of them signify a process that does not literally take place. Thus it is obvious that no physical poking is taking place when Internet users are poking each other on Facebook. Likewise, on hi5, users do not literally hit each other's hands when giving fives. Finally, Friendster users do not change their facial expression when sending each other smiles.

As for the intensional perspective, it seems that like *sign up* which means "sign up" despite the removal of "admission offices" from the situation SNS REGISTRATION, *poke, give five,* and *send smile* mean "poke," "give five," and "send smile"—i.e., what these expressions mean when used in real-life contexts—even though they do not refer to the physical acts of poking, giving a five and smiling. The reason for this is again the fact that as in the *registration*-example, the just named referential differences concern the non-core element Manner which specifies how we, e.g., poke each other on Facebook and how we perform this action in the real-world. (In the latter case we poke *by touching another person with our fingers*; in the former case—*by sending her/him a poke message*.) However, as far as the core elements are concerned, it is not difficult to see that both events involve (1) the poker, i.e., a person who either touches another person with her/his fingers or sends that person a poke message; and (2) the recipient of these actions.

In the rest of the chapter, we will try to establish whether we are right in hypothesizing that the SNS-related senses of *poke, give five,* and *send smile* are identical with those signified by these expressions in real-life contexts. We will start with Facebook pokes.

6.1.1. Pokes

To begin with, let us again consider the Facebook answer to the FAQ "What is a poke?":

> The poke feature can be used for a variety of things on Facebook. For instance, you can poke your friends to say hello. If you poke a user who normally does not have access to your profile, they will be able to temporarily see your Basic Info, Work Info, and Education Info. When you poke someone, they will receive a poke alert on their home page.
> http://www.facebook.com/help/question.php?id=124498

Given this description, the following conclusions can be drawn. First of all, from the intensional point of view, poking on Facebook is indeed not different from poking in real-life. This is because the above description is a pragmatic definition of how the poke feature can be used—*You can poke your friends to say hello*—but not a semantic definition of what the word *poke* means, e.g., *To poke somebody on Facebook means to greet another user* or something of the sort. The absence of the latter suggests that *poke* means "poke," i.e., a semantic definition is superfluous here because, as understood by facebook.com, *poke* does not signify different concepts when used to refer to poking on Facebook and poking in real-life.

Second, given the sentence *For instance, you can poke your friends to say hello*, it can be argued that "poking friends to say hello" represents the prototypical Facebook poking, i.e., the prototypical use of this feature by Facebook users. We are justified in arriving at this conclusion because, as mentioned in the previous chapter, conceptual categories are structured around their best representatives (prototypes) serving as their cognitive reference points. Linguistically, this is manifested in the metonymies CATEGORY FOR PROTOTYPE (e.g., BIRD FOR ROBIN) and PROTOTYPE FOR AN ENTIRE CATEGORY (e.g., FRIEND1 FOR SOCIAL NETWORK). Accordingly, the fact that "greeting friends" was chosen for the explanation of how Facebook members use the poke feature may indicate that "poking friends to say hello" is perceived as the prototypical member of the conceptual category POKING ON FACEBOOK.

Finally, as can be inferred from the third sentence, there are two different kinds of poking friends to say hello. First of all, we can poke existing FRIENDS2—i.e., already-members of our friends lists. On the other hand, however, we can poke all other Facebook users—both acquaintances and non-acquaintances—in order to initiate a contact. Indeed, when we poke users who normally do not have access to our profiles, they will be able to temporarily see our Basic Info, Work Info, and Education Info. In other words, when user A pokes user B, the latter gets access to an important part of the hidden profile information of the former. In this way, B can decide whether s/he is interested in communicating with A. By poking back, B confirms that this is indeed the case. By ignoring the poke, B makes clear that no such contact is desirable.

6.1.2. Fives

Now, consider the following definition of a five:

> A Five is a fun way to describe your Friend or express how you feel about your Friend using hi5 icons such as supermodel, classmate, hero, best friend, pretty, handsome, and lots more. A Five will appear on your friend's profile.
> http://tinyurl.com/dkrsx2

At first glance, it may seem that fives have very little in common with pokes: The latter are mainly used for greeting, the former—for describing other users. Particularly interesting is also that there are two different types of fives: (1) fives with which user A can describe user B, e.g., "champion," "chic," "cool," "cute," "nerd," etc.; and (2) fives that user A can use to describe the relationship connecting her/him with user B, e.g., "best friend," "classmate," "brother," "cousin," etc. (see screenshot 8).

As for the former type, it must be noted that here we are again dealing with the metonymy PEOPLE FOR WHAT THEY POST ON THE INTERNET which we discussed in connection with FRIENDS2. As stated in the previous chapter, one of the hallmarks of the Internet is that people are present there not in their entirety but by means of texts, photos and videos, etc., which they post on, e.g., their SNS profile pages. Hence, when hi5 users describe each other as *cool*, *cute*,

Screenshot 8. Fives on hi5

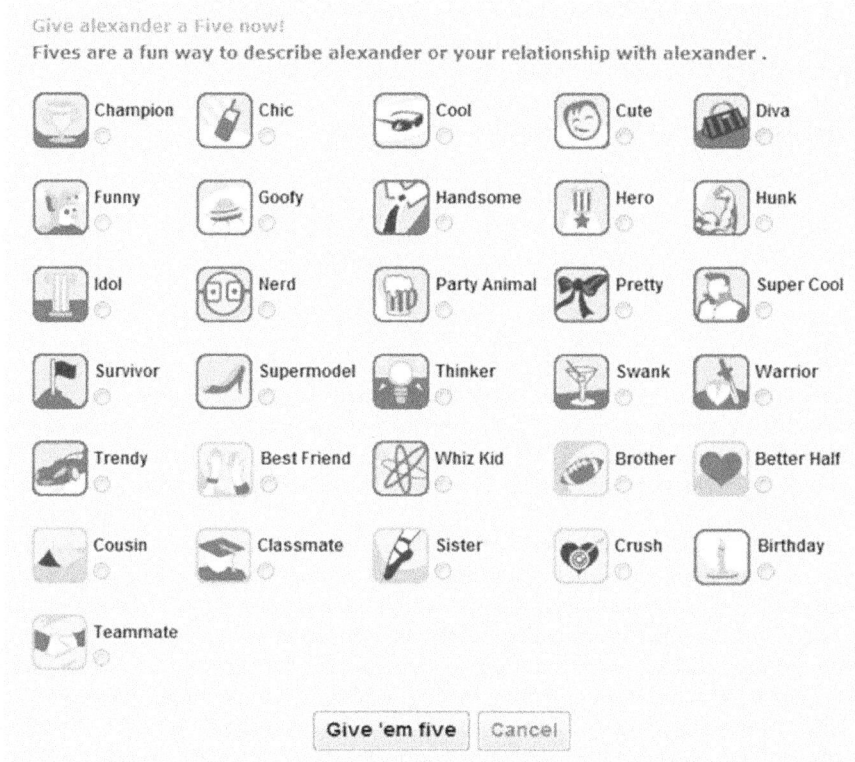

handsome, pretty, etc., they are most likely referring to other users' profiles (i.e., texts, photos and videos, etc., uploaded by profile owners), not to users themselves. That is, when user A gives user B the "cool" five, the motivation for this is most likely not that the "entire" user B is cool, but that, for example, a profile photo representing user B, according to user A, is cool. Of course, it is possible that users who know each other in real-life may use this type of fives in order to comment on what is part of their mutual discourse knowledge. For example, user A gives user B the "party animal" five because A knows that B is indeed a party animal. However, if user A and user B do not know each other in real-life, the "party animal" as well as all other *comment*-fives can only refer to B's profile, e.g., a profile photo on which B can be seen dancing, drinking alcohol, etc.

Given this fact, it can be argued that fives represent the network-specific alternative to profile comments. That is, instead of writing *Hey! Cool photo* or

You're a party animal, a "lazy" user can communicate the same ideas by giving another user the "cool" and the "party animal" fives.

The suggestion that a five is a special kind of a profile comment can also be given credence by the fact that in contrast to pokes, fives appear on users' public profile pages. Consider, for example, the "Stats" section:

Screenshot 9. The "Stats" section on a hi5 profile

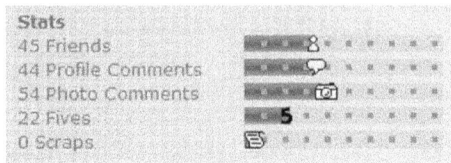

Among other things, it informs about the number of fives received by the profile owner. By clicking at "Fives," we also learn (1) which fives were given to the profile owner; as well as (2) who gave them. Likewise, by clicking at "Profile Comments," we learn (1) which comments were written; as well as (2) who wrote them.

From a linguistic point of view, the only difference between a comment and a five is their syntactic structure: Whereas the former usually consists of more than one "full" sentence—i.e., the one which contains the subject and the predicate as well as other grammatical relations—the latter is, strictly speaking, not even an elliptical sentence but a quasi-predicate (in the sense of Mel'čuk 2004: 8). That is, a noun or an adjective having a predicative meaning. For example, "cool" (you/your photo) = *Your photo is cool*; "party animal" (you) = *you're a party animal*; "best friend" (you; I) = *you're my best friend*, etc. In other words, when user B receives the "cool," the "party animal," the "best friend," or any other five, s/he has to translate them into the full sentences *You're cool!*, *You're a party animal*, *You're my best friend*, etc. These transformations are possible because, as just said, the lexemes *cool, party animal, best friend*, and all other fives are quasi-predicates. That is, the concepts COOL and PARTY ANIMAL cannot exist without an entity which is cool or a party animal, whereas the concept of a best friend requires the existence of two people one of whom considers the other her/his best friend.

However, it is obvious that this linguistic difference is the consequence of the technical difference between comments and fives: The former allow users to write their own comments, whereas the latter are already-written one-word comments from which users only have to choose.

Now, let us also consider the other type of fives—fives which hi5 users can use for describing the relationship connecting them with other users. As hinted above, from the technical point of view, *comment*-fives are in no respect different from *relationship*-fives. Both appear on users' public profile pages and can therefore be considered profile comments. However, from the point of view of semantics, it is only *comment*-fives which can be used as profile comments. Thus the "party animal" or any other *comment*-five can mean either that (1) A considers B a party animal because A knows this from her/his own real-life experience: A attends the same parties as B; or that (2) A thinks that B is a party animal because of numerous party photos posted by B on her/his profile. But the same cannot be said about *relationship*-fives.

Consider, for example, the "best friend" five. In contrast to the "party animal," the "best friend" can only mean that user A considers user B her/his best friend because in the real-world B is indeed A's best friend. It cannot mean that A considers B her/his best friend only because there is something on B's profile (e.g., a photo or a blog post) which, like B's party photos suggesting that B is a party animal, may suggest that B is A's best friend. Likewise, the "classmate," the "teammate," the "cousin," as well as the rest of the *relationship*-fives do not refer to user B's profile but to offline experiences of being classmates, teammates, cousins, etc., shared by both A and B.

In addition to this, the two types of fives differ with regard to the number and (more important) character of the semantic actants (see Mel'čuk, ibid.) required by their predicative meanings. As stated above, both *comment-* and *relationship-*fives are quasi-predicates—nouns and adjectives which, similar to verbs, denote events (e.g., the "birthday" five = user A wishes user B a happy birthday), states (e.g., the "classmate" five = user B is user A's classmate), perceptions (e.g., the "cool" five = user A thinks that user B is cool), etc.—and therefore cannot exist on their own, i.e., without the semantic actants representing the participants of the situations—entities to be referred to as *cool, party animal, classmate,* etc.—signified by them. However, it is clear that a *comment*-five like "cool" requires only one semantic actant: user B (or a photo representing her/him) to be called *cool*. A *relationship*-five, by contrast, requires two actants: user A and user B both of whom are participants of a particular real-life relationship (e.g., friendship, classmate-ship, cousin-ship, etc.).

More important, however, is that an actant of a *relationship*-five can only be a person (i.e., user B), not a non-animate entity such as texts or photos representing that person. Indeed, whereas the label *cool* as well as some other *comment*-fives can apply to both a person and a photo on which that person can be seen—for example, we can say both *You're cool* and *Your photo is cool*—*relationship*-fives allow animate actants only. That is, only user B her/himself, not her/his photo, can be referred to as *classmate, best friend, teammate,* etc. Cf., e.g., *John is my classmate* versus *John's photo is my classmate****Accordingly, if *relationship*-fives disallow non-animate entities as semantic actants, they can only refer to users themselves, not to photos on which users can be seen.

Having established in which respects a *comment*-five is different from a *relationship*-five, let us finally discuss the pragmatics of a five. Why do hi5 users describe each other as *cool*, *cute*, *party animal*, *best friend*, etc.? Unfortunately, in contrast to the pragmatic definition of a poke—*The poke feature can be used for a variety of things on Facebook. For instance, you can poke your friends to say hello*—no such definition of a five was available to me at the moment of writing. The only thing we know is that a five is a fun way to describe our FRIENDS2 or express how we feel about them. This, however, is a semantic definition of what *five* means, not a pragmatic definition of how this feature is supposed to be used. The absence of a pragmatic definition may, however, indicate that the pragmatics of fives does not or only insignificantly differs from that of real-life utterances containing the corresponding five-lexemes: *Your photo is cool!*, *You are my classmate*, *You are my best friend*, etc. This is especially true of those hi5 users who know each other in real-life. Thus there seems to be no difference between, e.g., the "cool" five given by user A to user B as a comment on B's profile photo and the sentence *This photo is cool* said by A to B as a comment on B's photo shown by B to A in real-life.

In the case of users-non-acquaintances, the situation is perhaps slightly different. Consider, for example, the "cool" five given by user A to user B whom A does not know in real-life. Although it is theoretically possible that A can do so just in order to compliment on B's photo which s/he finds cool, much more likely, however, is that the motivation for this is A's wish to initiate a contact, i.e., to attract B's attention in hope that B would "five back." In this regard, it should be noted that hi5.com is aware of the possibility of such use of fives and allows users to block fives sent by users who are not FRIENDS2 (i.e., users can choose the option "I am receiving fives from my friends only").

6.1.3. SuperFives

Before turning to Friendster smiles, let us also consider the SuperFive application which was mentioned in Chapter 4. Similar to "simple" fives, SuperFives also appear on users' profile pages and can therefore be considered profile comments. The only technical difference is that the latter can only be sent to an existing FRIEND2, whereas the former can be given to all hi5 users provided that the recipient has chosen the option "I am receiving fives from all users."

However, as regards linguistics, one can easily detect a number of differences distinguishing a five from a SuperFive. First of all, in contrast to fives, SuperFives are not quasi-predicates but predicates proper: That is, action verbs like *hug*, *kick*, *tickle*, *pinch*, *kiss*, *pet*, etc. (see screenshot 10). Thus, as argued by the developers of the SuperFive application, only SuperFives (not "same old fives") can "do stuff" to other users.

Screenshot 10. SuperFives on hi5

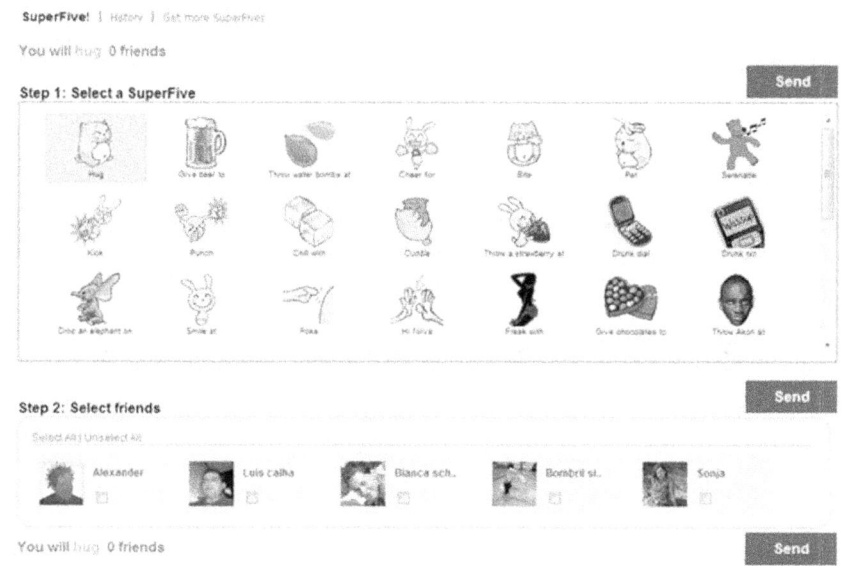

In connection with "doing stuff," there arises the question of whether the developers sincerely believe that by SuperFiving with "hug," "kiss," "tickle," etc., hi5 users do indeed hug, kiss, tickle, etc., each other. Or to put it differently, what do all these SuperFive lexemes mean when used in this way?

On the one hand, it may seem that none of these expressions can mean what they literally stand for since none of the actions denoted by them is literally taking place when hi5 users SuperFive each other. On the other hand, given that like in *sign up* and *poke*, referential differences concern only the non-core element Manner of SuperFiving (e.g., in the real-world we kiss *by physically kissing another person*; on hi5—*by giving the SuperFive "kiss"*), we can hypothesize that the reverse is the case. All SuperFives mean what they literally stand for.

The latter suggestion can be supported by the fact that SuperFives do not only consist of words like *hug, slap, tickle*, etc., but also of animated icons which are, to a very large extent, motivated by the literal meaning of an underlying Super-Five lexeme. For example, in the SuperFive "kiss," we see two faces kissing each other. The SuperFive "tickle" shows a bird being tickled by a feather. The

SuperFives "give beer/flowers" are accompanied by the beer and flowers icons. And so on.

Given this, it can be concluded that the meanings of all SuperFives do, of course, include the literal meanings of their constituent lexemes. In this respect, SuperFives do not differ from simple fives. However, the meaning of a Super-Five also includes an additional semantic component—"a particular emotion associated with the action denoted by a constituent lexeme"—which is less salient in the semantic structure of a simple five.

A good illustration of this is the SuperFive "kiss." According to the Oxford English Dictionary, in addition to meaning "a touch of pressure given with the lips [...] in token of affection, greeting, or reverence; a salute or caress given with the lips," *kiss* can also be used as a speech formula "forming part of an expression of affection written at the close of a letter, etc. (conventionally represented by the letter X)." From the intensional point of view, this means that apart from the conceptual meaning "a touch of pressure given with the lips," *kiss* has expressive meaning "affection." (If this were not the case, *kiss* would never become a speech formula "forming part of an expression of *affection*.") Also, this means that the utterance *kiss (you)* written at the end of a letter qualifies both as an assertive as well as an expressive speech act. That is, proceeding from the performative hypothesis (see, e.g., Cruse 2004: 355-357), according to which utterances without an explicit performative verb (e.g., *state*, *ask*, *promise*, *condole*, *thank*, etc., which can be followed by *hereby* and are used in the present simple tense, first person singular) can be performativized using an underlying explicit performative verb (e.g., *What time is it now?* = *I hereby ask you what time it is now?*), we can argue that *kiss (you)* can be performativized into both (1) the assertive *I hereby state that I kiss you*; as well as (2) the expressive *I hereby make known my affection to you*. In a similar way, Kövecses (2000: 2) argues that in the sentence *I love you*, "*love* is used both to describe and express the emotion of love" (which, from the speech act theory point of view, means that similar to *kiss you*, the utterance *I love you* can be performativized into (1) the assertive *I hereby state that I love you*; as well as (2) the expressive *I hereby make known my love to you*). And if this applies to *kiss* written at the close of a letter, why can it not apply to *kiss* used as a SuperFive? Indeed, as in the former case, the meaning of the latter seems to include both the conceptual meaning "a touch of pressure given with the lips" as well as the expressive meaning "affection."

The same analysis applies to the majority of other SuperFives. E.g., "hug" = (1) *I hereby state that I hug you*; as well as (2) *I hereby make known my affection to you*; "flirt with" = (1) *I hereby state that I flirt with you*; as well as (2) *I hereby make known my feelings* (e.g., *that I like you and want to flirt with you*); "slap" = (1) *I hereby state that I slap you*; as well as that (2) *I hereby make known my anger towards you*; etc.

In connection with this suggestion, it is important to note that in the case of "kiss," "cuddle," "hug," "slap," "punch," and some other SuperFives, the expressive meaning is already present in the intensional meaning of a constituent lexeme. The reason for this is that words like *kiss*, *cuddle*, *hug*, *slap*, etc., denote emotion-driven actions—usually, we kiss somebody in order to express our affection for that person—and therefore are so easily performativizable into expressives. Accordingly, the use of these SuperFives as expressives can be seen as an example of regular polysemy:

> Polysemy of the word A with the meanings ai and aj is called regular if, in the given language, there exists at least one other word B with the meanings bi and bj which are semantically distinguished from each other in exactly the same way as ai and aj and if ai and bi, aj and bj are non-synonymous. (Apresjan 1974: 16)

Thus, as we have established, *kiss* can mean both "kiss" and "affection." (The former as its conceptual meaning; the latter—as expressive meaning.) Likewise, it seems that *slap* used as a SuperFive does not only mean "slap" but "anger." Accordingly, given that the meanings "slap" and anger" are distinguished from each other in exactly the same way as the meanings "kiss" and "affection"—kissing and slapping are, as said above, emotion-driven actions, whereas affection and anger are emotions capable of triggering these actions—and given that the meanings "kiss" and "slap" and "affection" and "anger" are non-synonymous, it can be concluded that we have just discovered a pattern of regular polysemy EMOTION-DRIVEN ACTION FOR EMOTION TRIGGERING THAT ACTION.

This, however, does not apply to all SuperFives. Consider, for example, the SuperFive "give chocolates." Similar to all other SuperFives discussed above, "give chocolates" seems to be performativizable into both (1) the assertive *I hereby state that I give you chocolates*; as well as (2) the expressive *I hereby make known how I feel about you (i.e., that I love you)*. However, this impression arises not because of the literal meanings of the constituents *give* and *chocolates* (chocolates-giving does not always have a romantic connotation) but because of the heart box into which chocolates are placed on the "Give chocolates" SuperFive icon.

As for "same old fives," they also often allow both an assertive and an expressive interpretation. For example, the simple five "cool" = (1) *I hereby state that you are cool*; as well as (2) *I hereby make known how I feel about you* (i.e., *that you are cool*); "best friend" = (1) *I hereby state that you are my best friend*; as well as (2) *I hereby make known how I feel about you* (i.e., *that you are my best friend*); etc. Not accidentally, a simple five is defined by hi5.com as a "fun way to describe your Friend [e.g., *I hereby state that you are cool*] or express how you feel about your Friend [e.g., *I hereby make known how I feel about you: you are cool!!!*]." However, as stated earlier, in contrast to a SuperFive, the expressive meaning of a simple five does not seem to be more important than its assertive component. That is, it is equally important that (1) user A describes user B as *cool, best friend, better half*, etc.; as well as that (2) A expresses how s/he feels about B. With SuperFives, by contrast, much more important is that (2) user A expresses how s/he feels about user B; than that (1) A informs that s/he SuperFives B. In other words, given the already mentioned fact that none of the actions denoted by SuperFives is literally taking place when hi5 users SuperFive each other, the expressive meaning "I hereby make known how I feel about you" is undeniably much more important than the assertive component "I hereby state that I SuperFive you."

This conclusion may seem to be at odds with the developers' claim that SuperFives are capable of "doing stuff" to other people. Indeed, as already mentioned on numerous occasions, when user A SuperFives user B with, e.g., the "kiss," no physical kissing is taking place. At the same time, however, the claim that SuperFives are capable of "doing stuff" can be based on the expressive meaning associated with the literal meaning of an underlying constituent lexeme. That is, for example, by SuperFiving with the "kiss," user A does not "do stuff" to user B in the sense that A does not physically kiss B. On the other hand, however, A does do stuff to B in the sense that by uttering *I hereby state that I kiss you* (which the SuperFive "kiss" stands for), A expresses how s/he feels about B and in this way evokes a corresponding emotion in B: B is pleased to hear that A feels that way about B. This is the perlocutionary effect of the SuperFive "kiss," i.e., what hi5 users can achieve by SuperFiving with the "kiss."

6.1.4. Smiles

Finally, consider the definition of *send a smile*:

> When you click send a smile (located on a person's profile to the right of their main photo), a short message goes to that person's personal email and Friendster message page saying "Someone wants to brighten your day with a smile. Click on the link below to find out who is smiling at you!" If they click on the link they'll be taken to your profile page. Once you send a smile, it cannot be un-sent.
> http://tinyurl.com/dzvmrr

Like the definition of *poke* in 6.1.1., the above definition of *send a smile* is not a dictionary definition of what *smile* means (e.g., *A smile is a PM which Friendster users send each other in order to initiate a contact*) but a referential definition which describes what happens when Friendster users send each other smiles. Given this, it can be conjectured that the concept signified by *smile* in *send a smile* is "smile." Also, given the sentence *Someone wants to brighten your day with a smile*, it may seem that *smile* has an expressive component "wish to brighten another user's day." However, it is doubtful that Friendster users do indeed performativize *send a smile* into the expressive *I hereby make known my wish to brighten your day with a smile*. This is because, according to Friendster.com, the main pragmatic function of a smile is getting another user's attention:

Screenshot 11. A smile on Friendster

Send a smile
Get alex's attention and send a smile.
Include a message (optional):

Characters remaining: 500

send a smile   Cancel

Accordingly, apart from (1) the assertive *I hereby state that I send you a smile*, *send a smile* is also performativized into (2) the expressive *I hereby make known my interest in you*; as well as the (3) the directive *I hereby ask you to pay your attention to me* (e.g., *visit my profile page, send me a smile, add me to your friends list*, etc.). In other words, by sending a smile, user A makes clear that (1) s/he is interested in user B (the expressive component); and therefore (2) wants to initiate a contact (the directive component).

This, however, does not apply to all possible situations. Thus, if user B is already user A's FRIEND2, A does not really need to make known her/his interest in B since B is already aware of this. In this case, *smile* can only have a directive component: That is, user A may in this way signalize that s/he is eager to communicate with B (whom A has not seen/heard from for a long time).

6.2. Users

At the end of the chapter, let us turn to users. How do they understand the meanings of *poke, smile*, simple fives like "cute" and SuperFives like "kiss." To begin with, let us, first of all, consider the blogger Larry's explanation of "what is a poke on Facebook":

> So, you have heard about "Facebook", everyone is on it and having so much fun, but what exactly is it? And what is a poke on Facebook? [...]
> [...] a poke is literally a poke, like when you poke someone with your finger. The only difference is that you are not literally poking them but doing so on your computer and it will

> tell the person that you have poked them when they log in to their Facebook account. It may sound weird to be randomly "poked" by someone, but it is actually a lot of fun. It can also suggest a greeting, for example, if you don't feel like typing out a message to someone to say hello, you can just poke them! That way they will still know that you are there and willing to chat, you just didn't feel like typing! [...]
> You can even randomly poke people you don't know while browsing Facebook users, it's a great way to make new friends! Instead of sending the stranger a message, which could be rather awkward, just poke them! They might poke you back or send you a message and there you have it, the beginning of another great Facebook friendship!
> http://larry50.wordpress.com/2007/11/16/what-is-a-poke-on-facebook/

The conclusion drawn by Larry is identical with what we hypothesized above: *Poke* means "poke"—*a poke is literally a poke, like when you poke someone with your finger*—even though Facebook users do not literally touch each other with their fingers.

At the same time, however, it must be observed that not all Facebook users recognize this fact. Consider, for example, the suggestions that *poke* "doesn't really mean anything" or "means what you want to think it means":

> It's just for fun, doesn't really mean anything..like you could poke a guy you like for fun..it's kinda a flirty thing i guess.
> http://answers.yahoo.com/question/index?qid=20070513123559AA2MrLc

> A poke means what you want to think it means. Some people poke you because they think it's funny. Some people poke you because they like you. Some people will poke you to get your attention. Basically, there's no clear meaning to what the poke is, but it's just there to initiate conversation.
> http://tinyurl.com/d8ud5l

This, however, cannot be true. Let us begin with the suggestion that *poke* "doesn't really mean anything." From a morphologist's perspective, the claim that *poke* means nothing entails that *poke* is an empty morph—a morph which has a signifier but no signified (Mel'čuk 2001 [1997]: 18). But is *poke* really an empty morph?

The answer is, of course, no. One reason why *poke* cannot be an empty morph is that empty morphs discovered so far include (1) prepositions occurring in prepositional verb constructions, e.g., *depend on, wait for, capable of*, etc.; (2) personless pronouns used as subjects and complements, e.g., *It is obvious that, The rumor has it that*, etc.; (3) support verbs, e.g., *do a favor, take a step, make a decision*; and (4) interfixes such as, e.g., {s} in German *Liebesbrief* ("love letter"). It is obvious that *poke* belongs to none of these categories.

More important, however, is that if *poke* "doesn't really mean anything," it is not clear how users arrive at the pragmatic meaning of *poke*: *you could poke a guy you like for fun..it's kinda a flirty thing i guess.* How do they know that a poke is a flirty thing if *poke* does not mean anything to them?

Problematic is also the suggestion that "poke means what we want to think it means." If this were the case, *poke* would mean different things to different people. That is, different users would then have many different ideas for what purpose they poke and are being poked on Facebook. This, however, does not seem to be the case:

> What's a "poke" on Facebook?
> It can be either:
> a.) an intriguing flirting device (to members of the opposite sex)
> b.) a friendly joke-thing (to good mates)
> http://www.thestudentroom.co.uk/showthread.php?t=392796
>
> It's just a way to grab someone's attention.
> http://www.veganbodybuilding.com/phpBB2/viewtopic.php?t=13217
>
> Nothing really. It's just a way to grab attention.
> http://answers.yahoo.com/question/index?qid=20070424134857AA65AY8
>
> nothing at all, just something they came up with thats creative. i heard that when guys do it to girls it means something suggestive.
> http://answers.yahoo.com/question/index?qid=20070424134857AA65AY8
>
> Poking is just a cute way to tell someone that you are thinking about them. It's sort of like virtually poking their tummy with your finger. It's nothing sexual or whatever, it's just basically saying hi without words. I think it's cute.
> http://yedda.com/questions/poke_mean_Facebook_internet_7354431561140/
>
> Its also a good flirting tool...or a naughty flirting tool
> http://www.veganbodybuilding.com/phpBB2/viewtopic.php?t=13217
>
> poking a friend just means that. you poke the other person. for some, its a kind of friendship, for others it means you are flirting.
> http://answers.yahoo.com/question/index?qid=20070513123559AA2MrLc

As illustrated by these answers, the poke feature cannot be used "for a variety of things," as suggested by facebook.com. Instead, it can only be used for one thing: getting other users' attention, which includes (1) greeting existing FRIENDS2; and (2) flirting with other users whom one would like to "friend" and, possibly, meet in real-life. If *poke* "doesn't really mean anything" and if *poke* "means what we want to think it means," how can it be that so many users have the same idea of how this feature should be used?

The answer to this question is that for all these people *poke* means the same thing as for the blogger Larry: "poke," i.e., a touch with a finger. We are justified in arriving at this conclusion because both in real-life and on Facebook people poke in order to attract each other's attention. Accordingly, "getting another person's attention" can be considered the pragmatic meaning associated with the source concept POKING IN REAL-LIFE which Facebook users map onto the target concept POKING ON FACEBOOK. (In CTM terms, this would be one of the knowledge correspondences between the metaphor's source and target domains.)

However, as regards pokes as a *flirty thing*, the situation is different. Given that in real-life we typically do not poke strangers (even if we like them and want to flirt with them!), we cannot assert that the pragmatic meaning "flirting tool" represents an epistemic correspondence between the source domain POKING IN REAL-LIFE and the target domain POKING ON FACEBOOK. That pokes became a *flirty thing* is most likely due to the fact that from the point of view of technology, a poke is a PM—i.e., a message (although containing no words) that user A sends user B. If a poke is a message, it already has a very strong directive component "I hereby ask you to pay your attention to me." Thus, whenever we write e-mails, SMS, traditional letters, etc., we always want to attract other people's attention to ourselves. (And in contrast to poking, sending a message is a polite way of initiating a contact with people whom we do not know.) Also, since a poke is an already-written message (i.e., users do not have to write anything on their own; they only have to click at "poke"), it is far more convenient to poke a stranger instead of writing *Hi! Cute Photo! Let's meet tonight!* which, as Larry correctly points, can be rather awkward.

Presumably, all this is also true of Friendster smiles and hi5 fives. However, at this moment this claim cannot be backed by any empirical evidence. In contrast to *poke* whose meaning is the topic of a number of Facebook groups, blog entries, Yahoo! Answers threads, etc., the semantics of *smile* and *five* have not (yet?) attracted the attention of the Internet community. The reason for this is most likely the fact that users of these services are fully satisfied with the explanations provided by friendster.com and hi5.com. As stated earlier, the "Send a Smile" interface on Friendster contains the pragmatic definition of how this feature is usually used by members of the Friendster network: *Get another user's attention and send a smile*. In this way, the user learns that a smile is a message which s/he can send another user in order to initiate a contact. Similarly, the "five" interface on hi5 contains the creators' definition of a five as a fun way to describe another user or your relationship with her/him. Although this is not a pragmatic definition of how the five feature can be used, the user can nevertheless guess that (1) a five is a message whose content depends on the meaning of a constituent lexeme; as well as that (2) like pokes and smiles, fives can be used for getting other users' attention.

Finally, a few words must be said about how hi5 users understand the meanings of SuperFives. As in the case of simple fives, I have not found any discussions of what SuperFives mean or how they can be used. The reason for this, however, is not necessarily that hi5 users are fully satisfied with the explanations provided by hi5.com. The absence of such discussions can also be related to the fact that SuperFive (as well as all other third-party applications on hi5) has only recently been launched on the hi5 platform and has therefore not yet attracted the attention of a considerable number of hi5 users. Given this, let us take a brief look at how Facebook users use SuperPoke, i.e., a two year-old similar application which, like SuperFive, allows users to do "actions" (e.g., buy a drink, kiss, sucker punch, etc.) to their FRIENDS2:

Screenshot 12. SuperPokes on Facebook

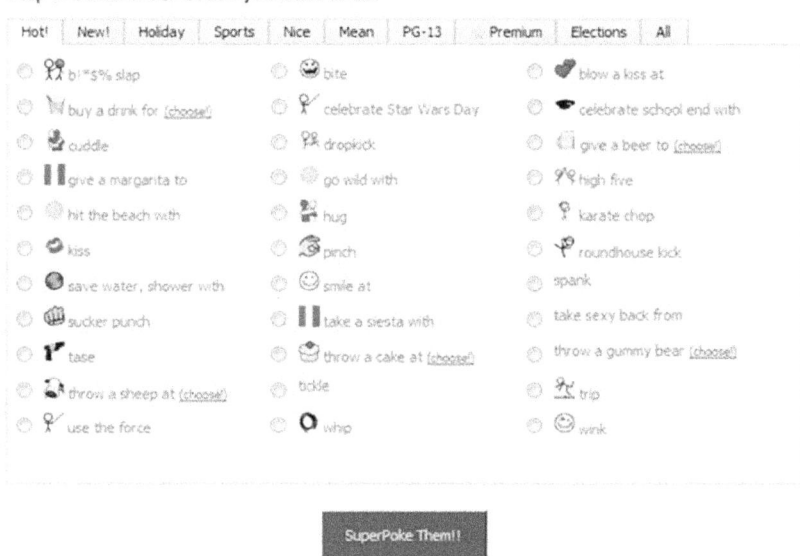

As for the meanings of these "actions," consider the question "What does superpoke mean?" asked by the user aimer:

> I am not facebook user but I noticed some girls superpoked my boyfriend several times.
> she has thrown cheesecake, danced, serenade him.
> auh my boy friend then baked cake for her.
> what are those meanings?
> Is this guy cheating on me???
> http://answers.yahoo.com/question/index?qid=20070513123559AA2MrLc

Similarly, the user Lorny asks the Internet community whether her boyfriend who SuperPoked another girl with "caress" is cheating on her:

> What does it mean if your boyfriend has friends that are girls, and on facebook using superpoke (an application that you can put on your facebook and do anything like cuddle, high five, etc) he caressed one of his friends and i want to [know] if he is cheating on me?
> http://www.answerbag.com/q_view/499037

Likewise, the user Indiana J does not know how seriously she should take her husband's use of the SuperPokes "serenade" and "blow a kiss":

> I recently joined Facebook as a friend of mine was going off travelling and wanted to stay in touch. My husband caught on to the idea and joined too.
> The problem I have is that I have been noticing more and more that he has been getting "poked" and "superpoked" by girls – and he has been "serenading" and "blowing kisses" with these girls etc.
> http://id.answers.yahoo.com/question/index?qid=20080210045901AA9lFzo

In this connection, let us consider the following question: Why do aimer, Lorny, and Indiana J worry that their beloveds sent these SuperPokes to other women if they know that the actions of baking a cake, caressing, serenading, and blowing a kiss did not literally take place? The answer can only be that for them, *bake a cake*, *caress*, *serenade*, and *blow a kiss* mean "bake a cake," "caress," "serenade," and "blow a kiss"—that is, what these words literally stand for. However, since literal interpretations are not possible, they conclude that in this way, their boyfriends/husbands expressed their feelings towards other women. (Recall the metonymy EMOTION-DRIVEN ACTION FOR EMOTION TRIGGERING THAT ACTION.) Thus if aimer's boyfriend "baked a cake" for a girl who "serenaded" him, it is possible that the SuperPoke "bake a cake" metonymically stands for tenderness which he feels towards that girl.

6.3. Summary

In this chapter, we have attempted to analyze the referential, the conceptual, and the pragmatic meanings of Facebook pokes and SuperPokes, hi5 fives and SuperFives, and Friendster smiles. The results can be summarized as follows. First of all, from the referential point of view, pokes/SuperPokes, fives/SuperFives, and smiles are messages which users of these services send each other. However, whereas pokes and smiles are PMs, fives, SuperFives, and SuperPokes are public messages and can therefore be considered profile comments.

As for their intensional semantics, the lexemes *poke* and *smile* as well as fives "cool," "cute," etc., SuperFives "kiss," "cuddle," etc., and SuperPokes "bake a cake," "throw a sheep," etc., do indeed mean what they literally stand for, even though actions denoted by them are not literally taking place. The reason for this is that referential differences concern only the non-core element Manner which specifies how these actions are performed in real-life and in the context of an online SNS.

As for the pragmatic meaning, we have established that pokes/SuperPokes, fives/SuperFives, and smiles are used for essentially the same purpose: getting other users' attention, which includes (1) greeting existing FRIENDS2; and (2) flirting (with both strangers and already-FRIENDS2). The pragmatic meaning "getting another user's attention" can be arrived at in three ways. First of all, in the case of pokes, users map their knowledge about real-life poking onto the use of the poke feature on Facebook: Both in real-life and on Facebook, we poke other people in order to get their attention. Second, given the users' conscious awareness that no literal poking, smiling, kissing, cuddling, baking a cake, etc., is taking place, these expressions are interpreted via the metonymy ACTION FOR EMOTION CAPABLE OF TRIGGERING THAT ACTION, e.g., KISS FOR AFFECTION. And finally, given that from the technical point of view, pokes/SuperPokes, fives/SuperFives, and smiles are messages which have a strong directive component by virtue of being messages, it is not surprising that they can be used as attention grabbers and flirting tools.

PART 3   FOLKSONOMIES

7. Tagging

As mentioned in the Introduction, the defining characteristic of a folksonomic Web site is collaborative tagging—the practice whereby users assign keywords of their own choice to the content (e.g., URLs of favorite Web pages bookmarked with an SB like Delicious, videos uploaded on YouTube, photos published on Flickr, etc.) which they want to make findable for other users. Particularly important is also that many folksonomic services allow users to subscribe to tags, i.e., be automatically notified about the availability of new content relating to a particular tag. (I will enlarge on this in the next chapter.)

In contrast to the previous case studies, the focus of this chapter will be not the term *tag* itself which can be considered a metaphor only from a diachronic point of view (see the last section of this chapter), but on conceptual metaphors which tagging has given rise to. We will start with tag clouds.

7.1. Tag clouds

As you can see below, a tag cloud is a list of tags (occurring on a particular Web site) where the size of a tag reflects its popularity, i.e., the more items are tagged with it, the larger the size.

Screenshot 13. Tag cloud on Flickr

All time most popular tags

africa amsterdam animals architecture art australia baby band barcelona beach berlin bird birthday black blackandwhite blue boston bw california cameraphone camping canada canon car cat chicago china christmas church city clouds color concert cute dance day de dog england europe family festival film florida flower flowers food france friends fun garden geotagged germany girl girls graffiti green halloween hawaii hiking holiday home honeymoon house india ireland island italia italy japan july june kids la lake landscape light live london macro may me mexico mountain mountains museum music nature new newyork newyorkcity night nikon nyc ocean parade paris park party people photo photography photos portrait red river rock rome san sanfrancisco scotland sea seattle show sky snow spain spring street summer sun sunset taiwan texas thailand tokyo toronto tour travel tree trees trip uk urban usa vacation vancouver washington water wedding white winter yellow york zoo

Like *Web 2.0*, *tag cloud* is a semi-phraseme whose meaning "list of tags" includes the literal meaning of the constituent *tag* but not of *cloud*.

Particularly interesting here is not that *tag cloud* is an easily recognizable metaphor (because most of our knowledge about the source domain CLOUDS IN THE SKY do not apply to the target domain TAG CLOUDS), but the fact that *tag cloud* is a genuinely Web 2.0 metaphor denoting a genuinely Web 2.0 characteristic of a genuinely Web 2.0 Web site. What is meant by this is that tag clouds of folksonomic Web sites can be analogized to (and, of course, contrasted with) Site Maps of traditional 1.0 Web sites. As an illustration of this, consider the Site Map of the White House Web site:

Screenshot 14. Site Map of www.whitehouse.gov

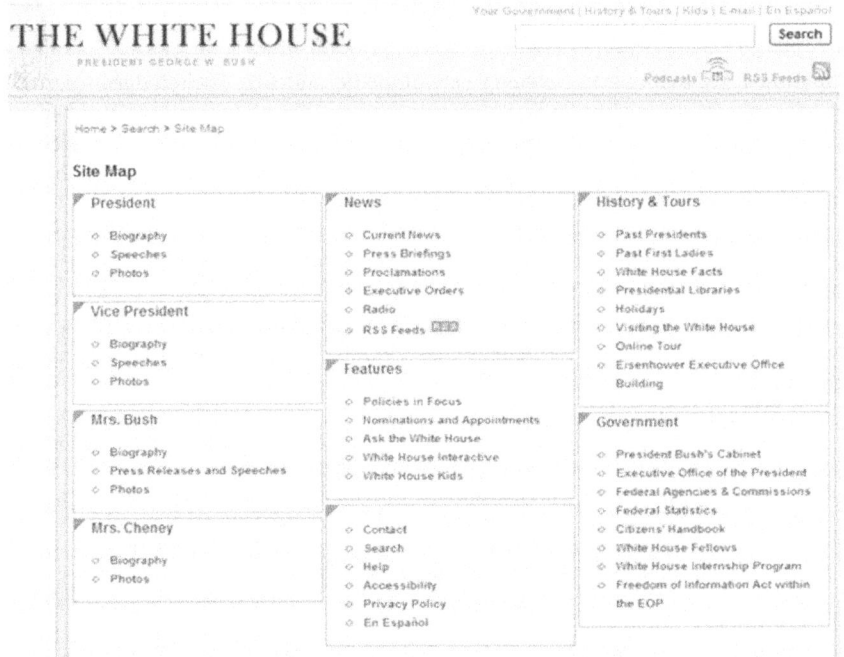

That TAG CLOUDS ARE SITE MAPS follows from the fact that both the former and the latter inform Web site visitors about the structure of a Web site. Indeed, both *architecture, birthday, friends, party, wedding*, etc., on the Flickr tag cloud and *biographies, speeches, press releases, photos, proclamations*, etc., on the White House Site Map are keywords describing the content of these Web sites.

Also, on both Site Maps and tag clouds keywords are simultaneously hyperlinks directing to Web pages containing the corresponding information. Thus if you click on, e.g., "Biography" on the White House Site Map, your browser will retrieve the "Biography" page of the White House Web site. Similarly, if you click on "wedding" on the Flickr tag cloud, your browser will retrieve the Flickr page containing search results for photos which Flickr users tagged with "wedding."

But, of course, there is an important difference: Site Maps are hierarchically-organized taxonomies of Web sites' content which are maintained by Web site owners, whereas tag clouds are folksonomies, i.e., non-hierarchically organized collections of all (or the most popular tags) occurring on a Web site.

7.1.1. Folksonomies = non-expert taxonomies?

The contrast between expert taxonomies (e.g., Site Maps) and folksonomies represented by tag clouds evokes an association with the well-known linguistic problem of the distinction between encyclopedic and folk knowledge—one the major apples of discord in lexical semantics.

Consider, for example, the meaning of the lexeme *salt*. As argued by Bloomfield (1933: 139), *salt* means "sodium chloride," i.e., the atomic formula of the referent of *salt*. This is an example of encyclopedic approach to meaning in which it is equated with the scientific knowledge about the referent denoted by the lexeme in question. But what about people who do not know the atomic structure of salt but nevertheless use the word *salt* to refer to salt (i.e., to a white substance used to add a salty flavor to food)? Don't they know what *salt* means? The answer is, of course, no because, as Ogden and Richards (1923) correctly point out,

> [b]etween the symbol and the referent there is no relevant relation other than the indirect one, which consists in its being used by someone to stand for a referent. Symbol and Referent, this is to say, are not connected directly (and when, for grammatical reasons, we imply such a relation, it will merely be an imputed, as opposed to a real relation) [...].
> It may appear unnecessary to insist that there is no direct connection between say 'dog,' the word, and certain common objects in our streets, and that the only connection which holds is that which consists in our using the word when we refer to the animal. (pp. 11-12)

But if there is no "direct connection" between the symbol and the referent—for example, between the word *dog* and "certain common objects in our streets" or between the word *salt* and the white substance which we use in order to add a salty flavor to food—it is clear that lexical meaning is not necessarily based on encyclopedic knowledge about the referent.

Or consider the true and popular etymologies of the idiom *kick the bucket*. According to the Oxford English Dictionary, the idiom *kick the bucket* acquired the meaning "die" because in the 16th century England the word *bucket* stood for a beam or yoke on which slaughtered pigs were hung by their heels. That is, when pigs were slaughtered, they were literally kicking a bucket (i.e., a beam or yoke) on which they were hung by their heels. This is the true etymology of the idiom *kick the bucket* explaining how it came to mean "die." But what about Present-Day-English?

Since *bucket* no longer means "the beam on which a pig is suspended after it has been slaughtered," speakers of Present-Day-English (who do not know the true etymology) can no longer establish a semantic connection between the concept of dying and that of a slaughtered pig kicking a beam on which it is hung by its heels. At the same time, however, at least some speakers can establish a connection between the literal concept of kicking a bucket and that of dying: Kicking a bucket may result in death if you stand on it with a noose around your neck:

> One theory as to why, albeit with little evidence to support it, is that the phrase originates from the notion that people hanged themselves by standing on a bucket with a noose around their neck and then kicking the bucket away.
> http://www.phrases.org.uk/meanings/218800.html

This is an example of popular or folk etymology, i.e., etymology arrived at by language users on their own, without recourse to etymological dictionaries.

But how is all this related to our discussion of tagging on folksonomic Web sites? The point here is that distinguishing between encyclopedic and folk knowledge (etymologies, taxonomies, etc.), we imply that the latter is not (or, at least, not entirely) true. That is, "committing a suicide by standing on a bucket with a noose around a neck and then kicking the bucket away" is not the true etymology of the idiom *kick the bucket*. Similarly, "white substance used to add a salty flavor to food" is not an entirely true description of the meaning of *salt*. A folksonomy of a tag cloud is not an entirely true description of a Web site's content. And so on.

But is this really so? Is "committing a suicide by standing on a bucket with a noose around a neck and then kicking it away" not the true etymology of the idiom *kick the bucket*? The answer to this question can be yes only from a diachronic point of view. From an etymologist's perspective, it is indeed true that *kick the bucket* acquired the meaning "die" not because some people used to hang themselves by kicking a bucket while standing on it with a noose around their necks, but because in the 16th century England the word *bucket* meant "a beam on which a slaughtered pig was hung by its heels." However, analyzed synchronically, the distinction between true and popular etymology does not make sense: There is nothing untrue or wrong in that some speakers attribute the idiomatic meaning of *kick the bucket* to hanging.

The same can be said about the distinction between encyclopedic and linguistic knowledge as exemplified by the two possible descriptions of the meaning of *salt*: "sodium chloride" and "white substance used to add a salty flavor to food." The problem here is that it is impossible to draw a clear-cut borderline between encyclopedic and linguistic knowledge since the supposedly linguistic definition "white substance used to add a salty flavor to food" is also based on encyclopedic knowledge about salt which, however, happened to be known by a larger number of people than "sodium chloride." Accordingly, the difference between the two definitions is not encyclopedic versus non-encyclopedic but more encyclopedic versus less encyclopedic.

Finally, consider the four tags to the photo "DSCF3599" from Flickr:

Screenshot 15. A photo of a KLM airplane on Flickr

As we can see, this photo is tagged with "s100fs" (which most likely means that the photo was made with the camera "Fuji FinePix S100fs"), "DUS" (which most likely stands for Düsseldorf), "Airport," and "Duesseldorf."

As a first approximation, it can be said that this is a very bad description of what we actually see on the photo since not a single tag is devoted to a KLM airplane, the seemingly central object of the photo. The consequence of this is that if we search for the tags "KLM," "KLM airplanes," or simply "airplanes" using the Flickr tag search engine, we will not be able to find this particular photo because the user has not assigned these or similar tags to it.

At the same time, however, it is clear that this seemingly unprofessional description has nothing to do with the user's unprofessionalism, but is instead related to the already mentioned prototype effect "order of mention" (i.e., more prototypical members of a category tend to be mentioned earlier than less prototypical). Thus the first tag assigned to the photo by the user Thomas Nick is "s100fs," which suggests that DSCF3599 was made with the camera "Fuji Fine-Pix S100fs." Accordingly, given the "order of mention" effect, it can be concluded that for Thomas Nick the most relevant characteristic of the photo is not that it shows the landing of a KLM airplane in the Düsseldorf Airport, but that it was shot with this particular type of a digital camera.

Or consider the tags assigned to the Web sites of the British and American National Corpus (BNC/ANC) by the Delicious users jstephen6672 and peachris. The former is described with the tags "vocabulary," "research," and "corpus"; the latter—with "linguistics," "american_english," and "corpus."

As in the case of Thomas Nick, these tags can hardly be called unprofessional or non-expert. Indeed, using jstephen6672's tags "vocabulary," "research," and "corpus," we can define BNC as a corpus which is mainly used as research tool by scholars conducting research on vocabulary. And using peachris' tags, ANC can be defined as a linguistic corpus of American English. The problem with these tags is thus not the unprofessionalism of jstephen6672 and peachris—users bookmarking Web sites like BNC or ANC are most likely either corpus linguists themselves or linguists doing research on vocabulary—but the incompleteness of the description of the two corpora. That is, in neither of the cases do we learn what kind of corpora we will be using if we decide to visit these Web sites: How many words do they contain? Are they based on written or oral texts? Are they synchronic or diachronic corpora? These are the most important questions relevant for the description of a linguistic corpus which, however, are left unanswered in jstephen6672's and peachris' tags.

In contrast, if you search for BNC using a traditional search engine like Google, you will learn that BNC is "a balanced synchronic text corpus containing 100 million words with morphosyntactic annotation." Given this, a genuinely expert set of tags for BNC should, in addition to jstephen6672's tags, also include "100_million_words," "synchronic_1990s," "written_and_oral," or something alike.

Of course, we cannot disregard the fact that a number of photos, videos, bookmarks, etc., tagged by users of folksonomic Web sites are/were/will be described with entirely wrong tags, i.e., tags that have nothing or very little to do with items which they are supposed to describe. (For example, Peters and Weller (2008) mention spam tags.) But the likelihood of this scenario does not seem very high since the main motivation for tagging is to enhance the findability of what is tagged. Hence, if I want other people to find the content that I tag, I will try to find the best possible tags for it. Accordingly, much more likely is the *in-*

completeness-scenario as exemplified by the above description of the landing of a KLM airplane and that of BNC and ANC.

Summarizing, a folksonomy (i.e., a tag cloud or just a set of tags assigned to a particular item) is not a non-expert but an incomplete description of a Web site's content.

Finally, it must be added that the term *folksonomy* is misleading because folksonomies are not taxonomies. Thus, as defined by Cruse (2004), taxonymy (spelled with *y*!!!) is a sub-type of the semantic relation of hyponymy relevant for classificatory systems. The hallmark of taxonymy is that

> a taxonym must engage with the meaning of its superordinate in a particular way, by further specifying what is distinctive about it. Take the case of *A strawberry blonde is a type of blonde*. The key distinctive characteristic of a blonde is the possession of fair hair, and *strawberry blonde* makes this more precise. Contrast with *?A blonde is a type of woman*. The key distinctive characteristic of a woman in the class of human being is her sex; however *blonde* does not serve to specify this any further, hence it cannot represent a 'type'. A similar contrast can be seen between *A mustang is a type of horse* and *?A stallion is a type of horse*: *stallion* specifies sex, but this is not a specification of what distinguishes horses from other animals. (p. 250)

As for taxonomy (spelled with *o*), it is usually defined as "the classification of organisms in an ordered system that indicates natural relationships" (American Heritage Dictionary) or as "a set of controlled vocabulary terms" (e.g., Leise et al. 2002).

Given these definitions, it can be concluded that tag clouds are neither taxonymies nor taxonomies. As for the former, tag clouds cannot qualify as taxonymies because keywords which we find on them are usually not involved in either the hyponymic relation of the *mustang: horse* type or any other semantic relation at all. As for taxonomy defined as "classification of organisms in an ordered system," we can, of course, argue that a tag cloud represents a classification of the content of a folksonomic Web site into items tagged by users. But, as just said, this classification is usually not based on similarity or any other semantic relation, so that it can hardly be called a classification in an ordered system. Finally, as for the second definition of taxonomy as "a set of controlled vocabulary terms," it must be reiterated that tags are not controlled vocabulary terms but keywords freely chosen by users.

7.2. Search engine metaphor

In contrast to the Site Map metaphor, the search engine metaphor does not relate to tagging in general but to the use of this practice by users of Social Bookmarks (SBs). That is, services like Delicious, Furl, StumbleUpon, Digg, etc., in addition to being social bookmarks, can also be considered a Web 2.0 alternative to search engines such as Google, AltaVista, Yahoo! Search, Livesearch, etc. As a linguistic illustration of this, consider the following comparison of SBs and search engines:

> There are many important differences between Search Engines and Social Bookmarking sites which we must consider. For example, Search Engines are not limited in how much information, or websites, they can categorize and store. They send out spiders, crawlers, or robots which follow links, take a snapshot of a web-page and store it in their database then move on. This can realistically continue forever. Instead, Social Bookmark sites are limited by the number of users they have in their network. If only 100 users are registered, only 100 users can add, rate and tag new web pages and the maximum amount of traffic you can ever get from that site is 100 people. Since Social Bookmark sites are updated by human beings, they are susceptible to intentional mishaps like spamming and misleading. They are also susceptible to trivial things like spelling mistakes and bias.
> Search Engines market on being able to provide almost any kind of information. They need to cater for the broadest spectrum possible in order to stay ahead. They need to be able to provide educational material for students, entertainment sites or videos, or whatever. On the other hand Social Bookmarking sites do not need to provide information on any particular subject or topic. While the majority thrive on the most attention grabbing, interesting information, i.e., videos, funny pictures, etc. Many Social Bookmark sites are specialized in areas like technology, programming, news & journalism, etc and may discard anything that doesn't relate to its particular niche.
> Search Engines will search and list as much of your site as they can, which is generally every single page which is linked from somewhere. Social Bookmark sites will only add one page or article at a time and only when someone physically submits and rates it.
> http://www.seanbluestone.com/social-bookmarking-sites-vs-search-engines

But given these differences and given that, linguistically, there does not seem to be a very close connection between SBs and search engines—that is, the term *social bookmarks* does not necessarily imply that SBs can be used in a similar way as search engines—what is the point of comparing SBs with search engines? The answer to this question is that SOCIAL BOOKMARKING WEB SITES ARE SEARCH ENGINES, i.e., there is something in the former that makes them similar to the latter.

Like all conceptual metaphors, the search engine metaphor is based on a partial mapping of the source domain SEARCH ENGINE onto the target domain SOCIAL BOOKMARKING WEB SITE. (By the way, the blog post above can be seen as a linguistic analysis of which of our knowledge about the source domain SEARCH ENGINE do not map onto the target domain SOCIAL BOOKMARKING WEB SITE.) As for similarities, both search engines and SBs allow users to search for keywords. This is the experiential similarity between the former and the latter allowing us to think of an SB as a hyponym of a search engine. (That is, an SB Web site is a kind of a search engine.)

Another important similarity is Web crawling and indexing. As mentioned in the post above, search engines "send out spiders, crawlers or robots," i.e., computer programs that search for the information on the Web and index it in order to make this information findable for search engines' users. As for SBs, the crawlers are users themselves who bookmark their favorite Web sites (i.e., store them in the database of a particular SB) and index them through tagging.

Given this description, it may appear that this fact is a dissimilarity between SBs and search engines. But this is only true from the epistemic point of view, i.e., what we know about Web crawling and indexing in the search engines context is not true of SBs. However, from the ontological perspective, this fact constitutes an ontological correspondence between the source domain SEARCH ENGINE and the target domain SOCIAL BOOKMARKING WEB SITE. That is, we can argue that the element "spiders and crawlers" in the source domain SEARCH ENGINES maps onto the element "users bookmarking their favorite Web pages and describing them with tags" in the target domain SOCIAL BOOKMARKING WEB SITE.

Like the homepage metaphor which we discussed in chapter 4, the search engine metaphor must have come into existence via the re-conceptualization of SBs as search engines. That is, the creators of these services have not (always) conceptualized SBs as search engines. (If this were the case, they would perhaps call SBs *search engines*, not *social bookmarks*.) However, trying to attract the attention of the maximum number of users, they integrated a number of items which are characteristic of search engines into SBs, so that the latter became similar to the former. Indeed, if SBs are social bookmarks, it makes sense to allow users to search for other users' bookmarks. And to improve search results, it makes sense to index bookmarked Web pages by asking users to tag them. As soon as these features were introduced on SBs, there appeared the experiential similarity between SBs and search engines, so that the former came to be analogized to the latter.

7.3. Intensional meaning

As for the intensional meaning, the word *tag* is less interesting than the expressions which were discussed in the previous chapters. Thus, as shown below, both users and creators seem to be unanimous in that *tag* means "keyword." (*To tag* is thus "to describe something by assigning tags to it"):

> Tags are like keywords or labels that you add to a photo to make it easier to find later. You can tag a photo with phrases like "catherine yosemite hiking mountain trail." Later if you look for pictures of Catherine, you can just click that tag and get all photos that have been tagged that way.
> You may also have the right to add tags to your friends' photos, if your friends set that option in the privacy settings for their photos.
> http://www.flickr.com/help/tags/

A tag is simply a word you can use to describe a bookmark. Unlike folders, you make up tags when you need them and you can use as many as you like. The result is a better way to organize your bookmarks and a great way to discover interesting things on the Web.
http://delicious.com/tag/

Tags are keywords that describe your group.
http://xat.com/alskefa

Tags are keywords, or should be, and any use of good keywords, tagged or not, helps search engines and searchers index your content better. It's not exclusive to tagging.
http://lorelle.wordpress.com/2007/10/08/are-tags-working-for-you/

This, however, is not a new meaning. Thus, according to the Oxford English Dictionary, a similar computer-related meaning "a character or set of characters appended to an item of data in order to identify it" has existed in English since 1948.

At the same time, however, it is interesting to note that this original computer-related meaning represents a metaphorical extension of the meaning "strip of leather, paper, metal, or plastic attached to something or hung from a wearer's neck to identify, classify, or label" (American Heritage Dictionary): Both senses share the semantic component "a description attached to something for the purpose of classification" and can therefore be considered polysemes. It is possible that for users who are not familiar with the original computer-related meaning of *tag*, the tagging metaphor is still alive. That is, the meaning "leather/paper/metal attached to something" serves as a motivating link for the meaning "keywords assigned to videos, photos, bookmarks, etc., on folksonomic Web sites."

In contrast, users who know that *tag* (as "a label assigned to identify data") had begun to be used long before the emergence of folksonomies do not need to recall that *tag* means "leather/paper/metal attached to something" in order to understand why *tag* can also mean "keyword." For them, the tagging metaphor is dead since it does not fulfill the additional naming requirement. That is, *tag* is the primary expression for the concept of a keyword assigned to an item of content of a folksonomic Web site and must therefore have lost its original metaphoricity.

96

8. Subscribe

As mentioned in the previous chapter, one of the advantages of folksonomies is that users can subscribe to tags, i.e., be notified about the availability of new content relating to a particular tag. Given this fact, it seems reasonable to devote a separate chapter to the semantic analysis of *subscribe*—one of the key Web 2.0 concepts. What does it mean *to subscribe to something on the Internet in the Web 2.0 era*? In which respects does this type of subscription differ from subscribing in the real-world (to, e.g., a newspaper or a Pay-TV channel)? And can we speak of the contrast between SUBSCRIPTION$_{2.0}$ and SUBSCRIPTION$_{1.0}$, i.e., the contrast between subscribing on the Internet during the 2.0 and 1.0 periods of its history? As in the previous case studies, we will start with the referential meaning of *subscribe*.

8.1. Extension

From the referential point of view, *to subscribe to something* usually means to use a special technology called RSS (Really Simple Syndication) (for which you need a special software called *feed reader* or *aggregator*. This, however, is nowadays usually integrated into most Web browsers.) If you visit a Web site that can be viewed by means of a feed reader and click on the RSS icon , your Web browser will open a feed page:

Screenshot 16. Education-feed on www.washingtonpost.com

washingtonpost.com - Education

Festivities, Anxiety Mark Kickoff Event
Saturday, August 23, 2008 6:00 AM

The morning began with the buoyant spirit of a pep rally -- all cheers, prizes and inspirational words from Mayor Adrian N

GMU Is Magazine's Leading 'Up-and-Coming' School
Saturday, August 23, 2008 6:00 AM

George Mason University tops the list of "Up and Coming" national universities in U.S. News and World Report's annual ra

As you can see, this particular Washington Post (WP) feed page contains (1) (very) short summaries of recently posted articles on the topic "Education"; (2) titles of these articles: these are also hyperlinks directing to WP Web pages where these articles can be read in full-text; and (3) the dates when these articles were posted on the WP Web site. In addition to this, a feed page can also contain a download link. In this case, we are dealing with a podcast, i.e., a feed page distributing audio/video content.

Particularly important about feed pages is that they allow users to subscribe to them, i.e., be notified anytime they change. For example, if you use Internet Explorer, you will be notified about the availability of new content via the bolding of a feed (in the browser's "Feeds" section):

Screenshot 17. Feeds on Internet Explorer

Also, it must be added that a feed page does not only contain summaries of newly posted items:

Screenshot 18. Feed options on Internet Explorer

As shown above, RSS is also a means of archiving Web sites (on users' computers). Thus a feed page with summaries of up to 2500 Web site's articles (posted at different times) can be seen as the Web site's archive (or, at least, the catalogue of that archive).

Now, let us proceed to folksonomies. As said in the beginning of the chapter, RSS can also be used for subscribing to tags on folksonomic Web sites. For example, if you want to subscribe to the tag "linguistics" on Delicious (i.e., be notified anytime another Delicious user describes a new bookmark with the tag "linguistics"), you have to search for the tag "linguistics" using the Delicious tag search engine and then, below the search results, click at "RSS feed for these Bookmarks." The same applies to photos on Flickr. If you want to subscribe to, e.g., the tag "Düsseldorf," search for the tag "Düsseldorf" using the Flickr tag search engine and then, below the search results, click at "Subscribe to stuff tagged with Düsseldorf." Finally, on YouTube, a tag can be subscribed to in the following way:

> To create an RSS feed for your favorite tags or users, simply enter the tag or username as specified in the below URLs. You can then add this URL to your newsreader. Please note, you will need to create a feed for each individual tag or user you wish to subscribe to.
> **Tags:**
> For example, if you wanted to create an RSS feed for the tag "monkey," you would enter: feed://www.youtube.com/rss/tag/monkey.rss
> **Users:**
> For example, if you wanted to create an RSS feed for the user "YouTube," you would enter feed://www.youtube.com/rss/user/youtube/videos.rss
> http://www.youtube.com/rssls?hl=en

8.1.1. SUBSCRIPTION2.0 versus SUBSCRIPTION1.0

In this section, we will turn the attention to SUBSCRIPTION1.0: If subscribing to an RSS feed is SUBSCRIPTION2.0 (i.e., the main way of subscribing to frequently updated online content in the Web 2.0 era), what is SUBSCRIPTION1.0? How was the problem of frequently updated online content dealt with in the early years of the Internet?

The answer to this question is the e-mail newsletter which even today is actively used for the same purpose on both 1.0 and 2.0 Web sites. (That is, on many Web sites, users can choose between RSS and a newsletter.) One of the main differences between subscribing to an RSS feed and subscribing to a newsletter is that the former does not require registration and is therefore more anonymous than the latter. That is, in the case of a feed, users do not need to sign up for it (i.e., provide personal information, choose password and username, wait for a confirmation e-mail, etc.). Instead, the entire SUBSCRIPTION event consists of only three actions on the part of the subscriber: (1) opening a feed page to which s/he would like to subscribe; (2) clicking at "Subscribe Now" (if s/he uses Mozilla Firefox), "Yes" (Opera), "Subscribe to the Feed" (Internet Explorer), etc.; and (3) giving a name to the feed.

In addition, using RSS is a more economical (in terms of the number of mouse clicks and thus time) way of checking the availability of new content. Thus, as a feed subscriber, the only thing you have to do in order to find out whether Web sites you subscribed to contain new information is to open the "Feeds" section of your Web browser. In contrast, as a newsletter subscriber, you have (1) to start your Web browser or the e-mail program you use; (2) sign in to your e-mail account by typing in your username and password; (3) open the inbox; (4) open each new newsletter; and finally (5) if newsletters contain only summaries of articles, visit those URLs where they can be read in full-text.

These and some other advantages of RSS are discussed by De Rossi in his 2003 blog post "The future of RSS – Is E-Mail publishing dead?":

> 1) **RSS is timely**. Subscribers get updates and breaking news as soon as they are published and not on the date the newsletter is due. RSS allows us to plug into selected sources of information, like independent reporters, researchers and industry analysts and when they disseminate or report some new information, it allows us to be the first to get it, without having to subscribe to any newsletter, or having to disclose our email address to a new, unknown company.
>
> 2) **RSS is cost-effective**. Cost of delivery and distribution is reduced dramatically. No more paying a mailing list distribution provider, nor having to format and layout news and articles for a different media than the website.
>
> 3) **RSS is standards-compliant**. (If wanted) Maximum compatibility is preserved allowing email subscribers with text, HTML, AOL or MIME Multipart preferences to all receive well formed news updates perfectly compatible with your email client.
>
> 4) **RSS is email independent**. Email client not required. RSS news and feeds can be easily read online, aggregated into a web page journal/portal, sent out to SMS clients or managed to create new online content.
>
> 5) **RSS can be fully integrated in your email**. Yes, no one forbids the final user from using new services and tools which do allow perfect integration and receipt of RSS feeds inside your email Inbox (e.g., NewsGator, BlogStreet, Info Aggregator).
>
> 6) **RSS facilitates organization of content**. Relevant messages can be easily archived, sorted and organized according to topic, in a fully automated way, something impossible with previously non-standard newsletters.
>
> 7) **The subscriber is again in full control**. Subscription and removal from a news feed is totally under the control of the user, unlike now where users may receive many newsletters that make it very hard or unintuitive to unsubscribe.
>
> 8) **RSS is private**. RSS subscriber never has to provide an email address to their selected information provider. Publishers cannot as a consequence easily resell those emails to unscrupulous marketers and email spammers. RSS is hardly spammable as you always know the source of each news item received, and there is no easy way yet to easily hack into the system.
>
> 9) **RSS is fully resuable**. RSS is a structured, re-usable content protocol that allows the content to be reused for many other purposes: feeding of other news channels and Web pages, integration into dynamic libraries and learning objects.

10) **RSS is searchable**. RSS can be fully indexed and searched just as Google does with the HTML content on the Internet.

11) **RSS is secure**. RSS cannot yet carry viruses or trojans like a newsletter or email attachment can. If it did, you could easily isolate and identify the source of your infection.

12) **RSS is modifiable**. Even after it has been sent out. Nobody forbids your ability to change a current posting, or revise an errata, and thus RSS subscribers indeed seamlessly receive that posted update. As a matter of fact, RSS posts can be also removed or expired, and while some would argue that this is not completely feasible, there is certainly a wide open opportunity to explore further in this direction.

13) **RSS will be seamless to use**. While not yet so, we are getting closer and closer to having news readers and aggregators fully integrated in email or so easy to use that it will not be a problem anymore suggesting their adoption to novice and non-technical users.

14) **RSS feeds are not blocked by spam and email filters**. As newsletter publishers know very well, the battle to overcome the spam barriers raised by spam and email filters is getting harder everyday while RSS-based news feeds have no such problem.

15) **RSS can be monetized**. RSS can support free as well as paid content distribution. Some publishers have already started text ads into their RSS-delivered news feeds. The good news is that if you don't like it, you can unsubscribe in a matter of seconds, without having to ask anyone's permission.
http://www.llrx.com/features/rss.htm

But, surprisingly, despite these advantages, e-mail publishing is still alive. Thus, as aforementioned, on many Web sites users can choose between the archaic newsletter subscription and the genuinely Web 2.0 RSS-based subscription. The reason for this is presumably the fact that RSS still "hasn't [...] caught on the mainstream," as argued by the blogger Steve M. in the post "RSS Mainstream?" published on April 04, 2008:

> I asked around the office and I asked some friends and family. Hardly a scientific study, but I just wanted to see what people I know thought about RSS readers. It only took a couple of people for me to see that most people have no idea what RSS is or what I was talking about [...]
> http://wouldbegeek.blogspot.com/2008/04/rss-mainstream.html

Part of the problem here is the semantic opacity of the abbreviation *RSS* or, being more precise, the fact that *RSS* is a quasi-idiom (Mel'čuk 1995: 183-184), i.e., a phraseme whose overall meaning contains the meanings of both of its constituents plus an additional semantic component inherent in neither of the constituents. A good example of a quasi-idiom is the phraseme *start a family* whose overall meaning "conceive the first child with one's spouse thereby starting to have a real family" contains the meanings of the constituents *start* and *family*, but, in addition to these meanings, also contains the semantic component "conceive the first child with one's spouse" which can be attributed to neither *start* nor *family*. Likewise, the meaning of the abbreviation *RSS* contains the meanings of its abbreviated constituents *really*, *simple*, and *syndication* (or *rich*, *site*, and *summary*) plus an additional semantic component "technology resulting in [really simple syndication] of often updated online content allowing users to anonymously subscribe to Web sites distributing such content."

The main "problem" with quasi-idioms is the unpredictability of their additional semantic component. Why should, for example, *start a family* necessarily refer to conceiving the first child with one's spouse and not to, e.g., marrying? And why should *Really Simple Syndication/Rich Site Summary* necessarily refer to RSS? This question arises because in the meanings of the constituents *really*, *simple*, and *syndication* or *rich*, *site*, and *summary*, there is absolutely nothing suggesting that the essence of RSS is the distribution of often updated online content by means of the so-called *feeds*. (By the way, the term *feed* is not very helpful either since it is a fully opaque, dead metaphor.) By contrast, the term *newsletter* is hardly idiomatic and fully transparent: A newsletter is a letter that contains news. Given this, it is not surprising that many users choose the archaic newsletter subscription instead of subscribing to an RSS feed.

8.2. Linguistic aspects

8.2.1. Why *subscribe*?

Having clarified the technical aspects of SUBSCRIPTION2.0, let us finally get down to the nitty-gritty of this chapter: the semantic analysis of *subscribe*. For this purpose, let us consider the following definitions of SUBSCRIPTIONRW, i.e., subscribing in the real-world. According to Cambridge Dictionary of American English, *subscribe* means "to pay money to an organization in order to receive a product or use a service regularly." The American Heritage Dictionary defines *subscribe* as "to contract to receive and pay for a certain number of issues of a publication, for tickets to a series of events or performances, or for a utility service." According to Merriam-Webster Online, *subscribe* means "to receive a periodical or service regularly on order."

Given these definitions, it appears that the major difference between subscribing to an RSS feed and subscribing in the real-world is that the former does not involve "subscription fees"—one of the obligatory participants of the situation SUBSCRIPTIONRW. As defined by Mel'čuk (2004),

> An element Ψ of the situation denoted by [lexeme] L is called its *obligatory participant* if and only if it satisfies the following condition: if Ψ is removed from SIT (L) [i.e. the situa-

tion denoted by L], then what remains either cannot be denoted by L or ceases to be a situation.

NB: "Removing Ψ from SIT (L)" is not the same as "omitting its lexical expression L(Ψ) from the corresponding sentence;" Ψ can be not mentioned verbally, but it still has to be necessarily thought of as present in the situation under discussion. [...]

The classical illustration is [*to*] RENT: *person X rents commodity Y from person Z for money W for duration T*. If, for example, T is not taken into account, the resulting situation is not *renting*: it must be called *buying*. On the other hand, if there is no W, this is not renting, either — this is *borrowing*. (In the text, owner, money and duration are easily omitted: *I rent an apartment in the downtown* is a perfect sentence; however, if I use the verb [*to*] RENT, I thereby imply 'from an owner Z for money W for a duration T'). (p. 10-11)

Proceeding from this definition, the situation SUBSCRIBING IN THE REAL-WORLD can be decomposed into the following obligatory participants: (1) subscriber; (2) provider/producer of the subscribed content; (3) content distributed by the provider to the subscriber (e.g., Pay-TV channels, newspapers, journals, etc.); (4) subscription fee paid by the subscriber to the provider; and (5) duration of subscription.

Each of these participants qualifies as an obligatory participant because its removal from the SIT (SUBSCRIBING IN THE REAL-WORLD) "destroys" the SUBSCRIPTION event. Thus it is clear that SUBSCRIPTIONRW is impossible without at least one subscriber. The same applies to the provider: If there is no provider, the subscriber will be unable to order the subscription. (Whom will s/he then send the subscription order form!?) And if the provider is simultaneously the producer of the subscribed content, the absence of the former (i.e., of the producer) will quite naturally result in the absence of the latter (i.e., of the content). (Who will be then producing the content!?)

Third, let us imagine that SUBSCRIPTIONRW does not involve "subscription fees," i.e., the provider allows the subscriber to freely access the content which it distributes. Will the resultant situation further qualify as *subscription*? The answer seems to be no. If the provider does not raise fees (because, for example, it is financed by the State), there will be no subscribers, i.e., people filling out the subscription order form requesting the provider to let them access the content which it distributes. (What is the point of preserving this procedure if subscribers pay no fees?) And as a result of this, subscribers will change into viewers or readers, i.e., people who view or read the content distributed by the provider without paying any fees.

Finally, since SUBSCRIPTIONRW is impossible without "subscription fees," it is clear that this situation is also impossible without "duration of subscription." Indeed, whenever we subscribe to something in the real-world, we are always requested to specify the period of time (e.g., six months, one year, unlimited period) during which we would like to receive the content to which we wish to subscribe.

Also, it must be noted that as in the *renting*-example discussed by Mel'čuk, not each of the obligatory participants of SUBSCRIPTIONRW must be present in the surface structure of a sentence containing the verb *subscribe*. For example, *I subscribed to Language* is a grammatically well-formed sentence, even though it does not mention (1) the Linguistic Society of America which publishes the journal *Language*; (2) the subscription fee; and (3) the duration of subscription. But despite their omission, these elements are nevertheless present in the situation described by this sentence, i.e., *I subscribed to Language* equals *I agreed to pay a certain amount of money to the Linguistic Society of America in order to receive the journal Language during a particular period of time*.

Conversely, both SUBSCRIBING TO AN RSS FEED and SUBSCRIBING TO AN E-MAIL NEWSLETTER consist of only three obligatory participants: (1) the subscriber, i.e., a user who subscribes to a feed or a newsletter; (2) the provider, i.e., a Web site allowing users to subscribe to its frequently updated content via an RSS feed or a newsletter; and (3) the subscribed content (e.g., summaries of articles, download links to audio/video files, etc.) distributed via a feed or a newsletter from the provider to the subscriber.

Neither SUBSCRIPTION2.0 nor SUBSCRIPTION1.0 involve "subscription fees." In the case of a feed, this is a priori impossible, given the anonymity of RSS. (How can providers raise fees if they do not know their subscribers!?) In the case of a newsletter, this is theoretically possible but makes very little sense since newsletters usually contain summaries of articles that are freely available on providers' Web sites.

Finally, given the absence of "subscription fees," it is understandable that "duration of subscription" is of zero importance for both SUBSCRIPTION2.0 and SUBSCRIPTION1.0 and is therefore not a part of either of the situations.

To conclude the section, let us proceed to its central question: How can the concepts of SUBSCRIBING TO AN RSS FEED and SUBSCRIBING TO AN E-MAIL NEWSLETTER be verbalized by the verb *subscribe* if they lack "subscription fees" and "duration of subscription"—two obligatory participants of the situation SUBSCRIPTIONRW?

To answer this question, it is, first of all, worth noting that in addition to the absence of "subscription fees" and "duration of subscription," there is another important (but less obvious) epistemic difference between SUBSCRIPTION2.0 and SUBSCRIPTIONRW. When we subscribe to something in the real-world, we always become owners of the thing to which we subscribe. This is especially obvious in the case of newspapers and magazines that are physically delivered to subscribers' mailboxes and become their property. In the case of Pay-TV channels, the situation is a bit different: We cannot say that subscribers become owners of programs and films to which they subscribe. Nevertheless, even in this situation there is something extremely untypical of SUBSCRIPTION2.0: the provider's commitment to guarantee the availability of the subscribed content. That is, if you subscribe to a Pay-TV channel, you expect to be always able to view that channel. But if you subscribe to an RSS feed of a Web site that often posts new content, you cannot expect to be always able to access that content. As mentioned earlier, a feed page usually contains summaries of (newly posted) articles or download links, whereas articles themselves and files that you might wish to download are located on traditional Web pages maintained by the provider. This means that if you click on the title of an article whose summary (in a feed page) attracted your attention, it may be the case that this article is no longer available on the Internet because the provider has removed it. This situation is often characteristic of folksonomic video and photo-sharing services like YouTube and Flickr where the uploaded content is often removed by the providers of these platforms if, for example, it contains pornographic material, violates someone's copyright, etc. But apart from these (and other) violations of the platforms' Terms of Use, photos and videos are often removed simply because users who uploaded them (due to some reason known to them only) decide that they should be removed.

Taking this into account, it can be argued that in the situation SUBSCRIBING TO AN RSS FEED, we are dealing with a double "deception": The subscriber "deceives" the provider that s/he subscribes to the provider's Web site (whereas in reality this, of course, does not take place: The subscriber *bookmarks* a Web site that frequently posts new content but does not subscribe to it.) But this "deception" is compensated by the facts that (1) the provider does not distribute the subscribed content in its entirety; (2) it does not guarantee the availability of that content; and (3) the content distributed by the provider cannot be *subscribed to* at all because it is freely available on the provider's Web site.

In addition to this, the use of *subscribe* in the context of SUBSCRIPTION2.0 and SUBSCRIPTION1.0 can also be attributed to two genuinely linguistic reasons. First of all, the expression *subscribe to an RSS feed/a newsletter* can be considered a linguistic realization of the conceptual metaphor SUBSCRIBING TO AN RSS FEED/AN E-MAIL NEWSLETTER IS SUBSCRIBING IN THE REAL-WORLD which, like all conceptual metaphors, is based on a partial transfer of the source domain SUBSCRIBING IN THE REAL-WORLD onto the target domain SUBSCRIBING TO AN RSS FEED/AN E-MAIL NEWSLETTER. And "subscription fee" is simply one of the elements of the source domain SUBSCRIPTIONRW that has no ontological correspondence in the target domain SUBSCRIPTION2.0/SUBSCRIPTION1.0.

But this leads us to the following question: Is there any reason for why it was the element "subscription fee" (and not, say, "content distributed by the provider to the subscriber") that did not take part in the mapping of SUBSCRIPTIONRW onto SUBSCRIPTION2.0/SUBSCRIPTION1.0? The answer to this question is that despite being an obligatory participant of the situation SUBSCRIPTIONRW, "subscription fee" is not an actant but a circumstant of the SUBSCRIPTION situation.

The contrast between an actant and a circumstant is traditionally described as internal versus external participant of a situation. According to Tesnie`re (1959: 102; cited in Mel'čuk 2004: 1), "*Actants* are beings or things that... participate in the process... *Circumstants* express the circumstances of time, place, manner, etc." (The contrast between an actant and a circumstant is very similar to that between a core and a non-core frame element that was introduced in chapter 3.)

Given the Tesnie`rian definition, it may seem, however, that "subscription fee" is not a circumstant but an actant of the situation SUBSCRIBING IN THE REAL-WORLD. Thus one can argue that "subscription fee" is a thing that (actively?) participates in the SUBSCRIPTION event in that it is paid by the subscriber to the provider. But this impression arises because "subscription fee" is part of the circumstant (or the non-core element) of Manner of the situation SUBSCRIBING IN THE REAL-WORLD. That is, in the real-world we subscribe *by filling out the subscription order form and paying the subscription fee*.

Summarizing, the situation SUBSCRIPTIONRW includes two actants: (1) the subscriber; and (2) the subscribed content; and three circumstants: (1) the provider; (2) the circumstant of manner including all entities and details relating to the *subscription*-procedure, e.g., subscription fees, subscription order form, etc.; and (3) the duration of subscription. As for the situations SUBSCRIBING TO AN RSS FEED and SUBSCRIBING TO AN E-MAIL NEWSLETTER, they include two actants: (1) the subscriber; and (2) the subscribed content (i.e., an RSS feed or a newsletter); but only two circumstants: (1) the provider of that content; and (2) the circumstant of manner including all entities and details relating to the *subscription*-procedure, e.g., Web browser, feed page, feed reader, registration form (in the case of a newsletter), etc.

The differences between SUBSCRIBING IN THE REAL-WORLD and SUBSCRIBING TO AN RSS FEED/AN E-MAIL NEWSLETTER are thus (1) the absence of the circumstant "duration of subscription" in the situations SUBSCRIBING TO AN RSS FEED and SUBSCRIBING TO AN E-MAIL NEWSLETTER; and (2) the different circumstant of manner: That is, in the case of SUBSCRIPTIONRW, the subscriber subscribes *by filling out the subscription order form and paying the subscription fee*. In the case of a newsletter, the subscriber subscribes *by registering for it* (i.e., *filling out the registration form, receiving confirmation e-mail, etc.*). In the case of a feed, the subscriber subscribes *by starting her/his Web browser, going to the feed page to which s/he would like to subscribe and clicking at "Subscribe."*

To conclude, as in the case of *sign up, poke, smile*, SuperFives like "kiss," etc., the referential differences between subscribing to an RSS feed/an e-mail newsletter and subscribing in the real-world affect only the non-core elements (or circumstants) of these situations. This is the explanation why both SUBSCRIPTION2.0 and SUBSCRIPTION1.0 can be verbalized by the verb *subscribe* despite the absence of "subscription fees" and "duration of subscription."

8.2.2. The bookmarking metaphor

Now, let us proceed to another source domain of SUBSCRIPTION2.0: the concept of bookmarking. As stated earlier, subscribing to an RSS feed seems to be much better analogizable to bookmarking a Web page than to subscribing to something in the real-world: The essence of both processes is saving the URL of a Web page which the subscriber/the bookmarker intends to visit again.

The suggestion that SUBSCRIBING TO AN RSS FEED IS BOOKMARKING can be proven by the location of the "Feeds" section in the toolbars/interfaces of some Internet browsers. As an illustrative example, consider Mozilla Firefox:

Screenshot 19. "Bookmarks" on Mozilla Firefox

```
Bookmarks  Tools  Help
   Bookmark This Page            Ctrl+D
   Subscribe to This Page...
   Bookmark All Tabs...          Ctrl+Shift+D
   Organise Bookmarks...         Ctrl+Shift+B
   Bookmarks Toolbar                        ▶
   NYT > NYTimes.com Home                   ▶
   The New York Times - Breaking News, World ...
```

As can be seen on the screenshot, Mozilla's "Bookmarks" (1) allows users to either bookmark a page or subscribe to it using RSS; and (2) stores both traditional bookmarks as well as RSS subscriptions in the same place. Also, in addition to placing "Feeds" to "Bookmarks," Firefox explicitly refers to feeds as *bookmarks*. Thus, as shown below, if you subscribe to a feed using the Firefox browser, you *add a Live Bookmark*:

> Whether it's news from CNN and the BBC, or posts on your friend's blog, the Web is updated continually. Firefox's **Live Bookmarks** feature automatically keeps track of these updates for you, so you always know when new content has been added to your favorite sites. With **Live Bookmarks**, the content comes to you. Instead of constantly checking Web pages for changes and additions, a **Live Bookmark** delivers updates to you as soon as they are available.
> http://www.mozilla.com/en-US/firefox/livebookmarks.html

Understood in this way, a feed can indeed be considered a live or a dynamic bookmark. A traditional bookmark is, by contrast, a dead or a static bookmark, i.e., a bookmark that does not do anything apart from storing the URL of a bookmarked Web page.

Given the FEED AS A BOOKMARK metaphor, let us consider the hierarchy of the conceptual metaphors SUBSCRIBING TO AN RSS FEED IS SUBSCRIBING IN THE REAL WORLD and SUBSCRIBING TO AN RSS FEED IS BOOKMARKING. The most interesting question here is which of these two metaphors represents the central metaphorical conception of SUBSCRIPTION$_{2.0}$.

The answer to this question is, of course, the subscription metaphor. The main reason for this is that it is the original metaphorical conception of SUBSCRIPTION$_{2.0}$. That is, RSS came into existence not because its creators wanted to replace static bookmarks through dynamic feeds, but because they wanted to find an alternative to e-mail newsletters in order to solve the problem of spam, which is reflected in the well-known fact that apart from "Really Simple Syndication" and "Rich Site Summary," the abbreviation *RSS* is often said to stand for "Really Stops Spam." Accordingly, subscribing to an RSS feed was from the very beginning analogized to subscribing to an e-mail newsletter, not to bookmarking a Web page. (As for the bookmarking metaphor, it must have come into existence in exactly the same way as the metaphors SNS PROFILES ARE PERSONAL WEB SITES and SOCIAL BOOKMARKING WEB SITES ARE SEARCH ENGINES, i.e., through the re-conceptualization of subscribing to a feed as bookmarking a Web page.) This is the reason why the concept of live bookmarking (i.e., subscribing to an RSS feed) is still usually verbalized by the verb *subscribe*, whereas *bookmark* remains reserved for traditional static bookmarking. Even Mozilla Firefox—the browser (1) where feeds are located at the same place as bookmarks; and (2) where feeds are called *live bookmarks*—uses *bookmark* to refer to static bookmarking; and *subscribe*—to dynamic bookmarking.

8.2.3. Intension

As for the conceptual meaning of *subscribe*, consider the following definitions:

> To become a member of. One can subscribe to a mailing list, a newsgroup, an online service or an Internet service.
> http://www.geeksnet.com/faq/glossary.htm#S

> The act of joining a mailing list.
> http://www.cstonecanada.com/primer/glossary.asp#s

> Used with mailing lists and newsgroups. When you subscribe to a mailing list, your name is added to the list of recipients for any mailings to the list.
> http://www.hyperglossary.co.uk/terms/defns2z.htm

Particularly interesting here is the first definition in which *subscribe* is defined as "become a member." Indeed, when we subscribe to something (both in real-life and on the Internet), we always become members of the group of people who subscrib(ed) to the same thing as us. For example, when I subscribed to *Language*, I became a member of the journal's *subscribers*-group. Likewise, when I subscribed to the journal's newsletter/RSS feed, I became a member of the group of Internet users who receive free online content distributed by the journal. Given this fact, it is not surprising that *sign up* and *register*—verbs which, as we established in chapter 3, convey the same idea of becoming a member of a socially defined group—can be used as synonyms of *subscribe*, especially when used in the context of SUBSCRIPTION1.0:

Sign-up for a Newsletter
Get the latest Alliance and industry news delivered direct to your inbox.
http://www.ciscointelalliance.com/news/newsletter.aspx

Users normally **register for a newsletter** on a website.
http://www.welie.com/patterns/showPattern.php?patternID=newsletter

These facts, however, should not lead us to the conclusion that the meaning of *subscribe* is "sign up" or "register." The difference between these concepts is that in the case of *subscribe*, the group which the subscriber joins as a result of her/his subscription is not an actant but a circumstant of the SUBSCRIPTION situation. That is, when we subscribe to something (both in real-life and on the Internet), we are usually not very interested in the fact that we become members of various *subscribers*-groups. (I, for instance, do not care at all about the fact that I am a member of the group of *Language*-subscribers.) Instead, we are interested in regularly receiving the product to which we subscribe (and for which we, in the case of SUBSCRIPTIONRW, are even ready to pay the subscription fee). By contrast, in the case of signing up/registering, it is often the group membership alone (and not the content distributed by the provider) that triggers our decision to sign up. For example, when Internet users sign up/register for SNSs like MySpace and Facebook, they are motivated by the wish to be present on these platforms (or, in other words, become members of the group of users of these platforms) in order to find and be found there by other people.

In addition to this, the term *register* (but, as far as I can judge, not *sign up*) connotes "obligatoriness [of registration]" that seems to be absent in the semantics of *subscribe*. Thus, in the prototypical case, we subscribe only when we want to subscribe (i.e., e.g., when the thing to which we subscribe can only be obtained through subscription). However, very often we register not because we want to register but because we are required to register. For example, in many countries of the world people are required to register as residents of a city where they live. (In Germany, for example, we have *Einwohnermeldeämter*, i.e., registration of address offices.)

Finally, given the technical differences between SUBSCRIPTION2.0 and SUBSCRIPTION1.0, it may seem that the use of *sign up* and *register* as synonyms of *subscribe* can only be possible in the context of a newsletter. Thus it is only SUBSCRIPTION1.0 where users are required to sign up by filling out a registration form, choosing a password and a username, confirming the registration by clicking at a confirmation link, etc. But, surprisingly, both *sign up* and *register* do occur instead of *subscribe* referring to SUBSCRIPTION2.0:

> To **sign up for an RSS feed** from PHAC [Public Health Agency of Canada]:
> - Click on the XML button for the feed you wish to add to your list; or
> - Copy the link below for the feed you wish to add to your list, then paste it into your RSS feed reader.
> http://www.phac-aspc.gc.ca/rss/index-eng.php
>
> You **register for an RSS feed** from a particular website such as nytheatre.com one time, and then new headlines and summaries will be downloaded to your computer automatically as they become available.
> http://www.nytheatre.com/nytheatre/rssinfo.php

As suggested above, these uses of *sign up* and *register* are technically incorrect since one of the hallmarks of RSS is the absence of registration.

Also, the use of *sign up* and *register* as synonyms of *subscribe* in the context of SUBSCRIPTION2.0 seems to be at odds with the BECOMING A MEMBER frame. As stated in chapter 3, one of the characteristics of real-life groups which register their members is the presence of "admission offices" whose task is to check whether new members fulfill "admission requirements" and, if yes, register them as new members. Likewise, Internet services where users are required to register can be said to have "admission offices" which register new users as new members. (Without, however, checking whether they fulfill all "admission requirements.") Thus if you sign up/register for an SNS like MySpace or Facebook, the platform of your choice will automatically register you as its new member as soon as it receives your registration form. Likewise, if you sign up/register for a newsletter, the provider of the newsletter will automatically register you as a new member of the group of newsletter recipients as soon as it receives your registration form. But what about RSS feeds? If you "sign up/register" for an RSS feed, the provider of the feed will not *register* you as a new member of the feed subscribers group because, due to the absence of registration, s/he will never learn about the fact of your "registration." So, how is it then possible to use *sign up* and *register* as synonyms of *subscribe*?

The answer to this question is that despite the previously named referential differences between SUBSCRIPTION2.0 and SUBSCRIPTIONRW, the conceptual meaning of *subscribe* has remained the same: In both contexts *subscribe* means "subscribe" and can therefore be replaced by *sign up* and *register*, even though in the RSS context this is technically incorrect.

As for the reason for the non-change of meaning of *subscribe*, it is identical with that of *sign up*, *poke*, *smile*, SuperFives like "*kiss*," etc. In the case of SUBSCRIPTION2.0, referential differences concern only the non-core element (or circumstant of) Manner which specifies how we subscribe in real-life and how we perform this action using RSS. In the former case, we subscribe *by filling out a subscription order form and paying the subscription fee*. In the latter case, we subscribe *by retrieving the feed page to which we would like to subscribe and clicking at "Subscribe."*

9. Channel

In the last chapter, we will deal with *channels*—personalized users' pages on YouTube, Veoh, and some other video-sharing services. As usual, let us begin with the referential meaning of the lexeme under consideration.

9.1. Extension

According to YouTube Glossary, "a channel is a user's page. It contains a user's profile information, videos, favorites, etc." (http://tinyurl.com/cqvqet) Similarly, YouTube Help Center defines *channel* as "a centralized location where other users can see your public videos, favorites, comments, subscribers, video log, bulletin status, and recent activity":

> **Getting Started: Channel/Profile definition**
> Everyone who has joined YouTube can view their personal information on their Channel or Profile page. It's a centralized location where other users can see your public videos, favorites, comments, subscribers, video log, bulletin status, and recent activity. Users can also see stats about you, like how long you've been a YouTube member, how old you are, and how many videos you've watched.
> Your Channel's an easy place for people to connect with you, to send you a message, share a channel, add you as a friend, or add comments to your Channel.
> http://tinyurl.com/d46sad

Reading these definitions, one can easily notice a remarkable similarity between a channel page on YouTube and a profile page on an SNS like MySpace and Facebook: Both the former and the latter contain (almost) the same items: profile information describing the channel/profile owner, friends list, contact information, v-log/blog, videos, etc. Both the former and the latter have personalized URLs (cf., e.g., youtube.com/johnmccain vs. myspace.com/johnmccain). Both the former and the latter can be easily customized by users with zero knowledge of HTML; etc.

At the same time, however, it must be observed that a YouTube channel differs from an SNS profile in at least two important respects. The first difference relates to the necessary and sufficient criteria distinguishing the former from the latter. As we established in chapter 4, in the case of an SNS profile, these include a $PROFILE2\_1.0$-like description of the profile owner and "Friends": These are the minimal requirements that a Web page must fulfill in order to qualify as $PROFILE2\_2.0$. (This is the reason why a channel page on YouTube which contains both these items can be considered an SNS profile page. This is the reason why YouTube is often referred to as a social networking Web site.)

As for a YouTube channel page, it seems that the only necessary and sufficient criterion is the section "Videos" containing the videos uploaded by the channel owner. This is because of the original intensional semantics of *channel*—the meaning "television station" which the creators of the YouTube platform have chosen as the source domain for the metaphorical conceptualization of a YouTube channel. Thus, as defined by youtube.com, YouTube is "a free online video streaming service" where users broadcast themselves:

Screenshot 20. YouTube symbol

Accordingly, if A YOUTUBE CHANNEL IS A TRADITIONAL TV CHANNEL, there can be no doubt that it is "Videos" (not any other item which can currently be found on YouTube channels) which defines a YouTube channel as its distinctive feature.

In addition to the different necessary and sufficient criteria, a channel page on YouTube differs from an SNS profile page in that it is only the former which distinguishes between FRIENDS2 and subscribers. As we concluded in chapter 5, "subscriber" is one of the meanings of FRIEND2. But on YouTube, SUBSCRIBER and FRIEND2 are two different concepts distinguished by the creators. Apart from this, subscribing to a YouTube channel does not require the approval of the channel owner. That is, once the user clicks at "Subscribe," YouTube confirms that "[her/his] subscription to [e.g., Barack Obama's channel] has been added." A friend request, by contrast, has to be approved of by the channel owner.

9.2. Television metaphor

Despite the obvious differences between a traditional TV channel which (in the prototypical case) produces and regularly broadcasts a number of programs of various genres (e.g., news, talk shows, series, etc.) and a YouTube channel which usually contains users' self-made videos, A YOUTUBE CHANNEL IS A TRADITIONAL TV CHANNEL is a very systematic conceptual metaphor in which a large number of entities associated with traditional TV channels map neatly onto the corresponding entities in the target domain A YOUTUBE CHANNEL.

First of all, like traditional TV channels, YouTube channels have names. For example, Britney Spears' YouTube channel is called *BritneyTV*. (The use of *TV* as a constituent part of the name of a YouTube channel—in addition to *BritneyTV*, there are also *TokioHotelTV*, *SampdoriaWebTV*, *HowardTV*, etc.—can, like the use of *channel* in the context of a YouTube channel, be considered a linguistic realization of the conceptual metaphor A YOUTUBE CHANNEL IS A TRADITIONAL TV CHANNEL.) Like traditional TV channels, channels on You-

Tube have "programs"—videos uploaded by channel owners—as well as viewers who watch them. Like Pay-TV channels, YouTube channels have subscribers. But particularly important is the mapping "broadcast → upload videos."

As stated earlier, on YouTube users "broadcast" themselves by uploading all kinds of videos on their channel pages and "sharing them" (i.e., making them viewable for) other users:

Screenshot 21. Broadcast options on YouTube

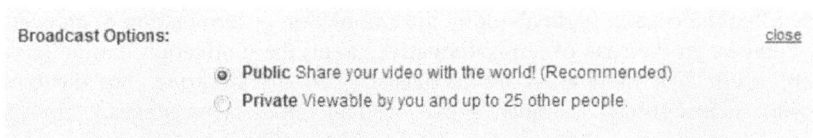

Particularly interesting here is that in addition to the quality of videos broadcast by a traditional TV channel and a YouTube channel, *broadcast* and *upload* are verbs which have very different aspectual meanings (or Aktionsarten).

9.2.1. YouTube broadcasting. Aspectual analysis.

As for qualitative aspectuality (i.e., which is concerned with the quality of an event, e.g., whether it is static or dynamic; limitative or non-limitative; perfective or imperfective), the most important difference is that *upload* is a limitative (telic, terminative, conclusive) verb, whereas *broadcast* has a non-limitative (atelic, non-terminative, non-conclusive) meaning. As defined by Xolodovič (1963; cited in Maslov 1978: 314-315), the defining characteristic of a limitative verb is that it denotes an action which ends in a transition to a particular state. For example, the action "uploading a video on YouTube" is usually followed by the state "the video is available on YouTube and can be viewed by other users." This state is the "limit" of the action of uploading (hence the term *limitative verb*) which terminates the action as soon as it is achieved. Particularly important here is that the limit of (the action denoted by) a limitative verb is very often the motivation triggering the execution of that action. Thus when an Internet user uploads a video on YouTube or on a similar Internet platform, s/he usually wants to make that video available to other users.

In contrast, the completion or, being more exact, the cessation of a non-limitative action does not bring about a particular state. What happens if, for example, a TV or a radio station ceases broadcasting? Very often the frequency used by one station is given to another station, so that it can start broadcasting its own programs as soon as the frequency is abandoned by the previous owner. This, however, is not the only possibility. In addition to this situation, the frequency abandoned by station A can remain free for a relatively long period of time (e.g., until the radio and television commission makes a decision to give it to station B). Or it is also possible that the termination of the event "station A broadcasts on frequency X" will be followed by the event "station A moves to a different frequency," i.e., very often TV and radio stations simply change frequencies on which they broadcast their programs.

The non-limitative character of *broadcast* becomes even more obvious if we compare the motivations for uploading a video on YouTube and TV broadcasting. As already mentioned, in the case of a limitative verb, the motivation is very often the state brought about by the completion or termination of an event. By contrast, in the case of a non-limitative event, the motivation is usually the event itself: The motivation for broadcasting is *broadcasting*, not the three possible states/events described above ensuing upon its termination. As was pointed out by Diez (1844; cited in Maslov 1973: 398), a non-limitative action "is not begun in order to be finished." Thus a TV station usually does not start broadcasting in order to cease doing this and, e.g., leave the frequency for another station, but to keep broadcasting as many years as possible.

Closely connected to qualitative aspectuality is linear or phase aspectuality. According to Plungjan (2000: 297), any event or situation can be decomposed into the following five stages or phases: (1) the preparatory stage (e.g., I am going to upload a video on YouTube/a TV station is going to start broadcasting); (2) the beginning: the transition from the state "the situation does not take place" to the state "the situation takes place" (e.g., I choose a video which I want to upload and click at "Upload"/a TV station starts broadcasting); (3) the end: the transition from the state "the situation takes place" to the state "the situation no longer takes place" (e.g., my computer finishes uploading a video/a TV station ceases broadcasting); (4) the middle stage: the stage between the beginning and the end (e.g., the moment when my computer is in the process of uploading a video/a TV station is on air); and (5) the resultative stage (e.g., I've uploaded a video on YouTube and, as a result of this, the video is now available there and can be viewed by other users/the frequency abandoned by a TV station is free). The preparatory and the resultative stages are traditionally grouped into *external stages*, whereas the beginning, the end, and the middle stage are known as *internal stages*.

Although, as shown above, each of these five stages equally applies to both *broadcast* and *upload* (as well as any other verb), not each of these five stages is equally important in the structure of the events which they denote. In the case of *broadcast*, the most important stage is the middle stage, the moment when a TV station is on air. The middle stage is the default aspectual meaning of *broadcast*, i.e., the meaning that can be expressed by *broadcast* only. Consider, for example, the sentence *KSCI-TV in Los Angeles* **broadcasts** *news and entertainment programming in several Asian languages* (Corpus of Contemporary American

English). It is clear that that the underlined *broadcasts* refers to neither the beginning nor the end of the event KSCI-TV BROADCASTS NEWS AND ENTERTAINMENT PROGRAMMING IN SEVERAL ASIAN LANGUAGES, but to the stage between them.

At the same time, however, if you want to explicitly refer to the beginning or the end of the BROADCASTING event, *broadcast* is not enough. Given the nonexistence of inceptive and terminative aspects in English (which in some other languages encode the initial and the final stages; see Frawley 1992: 321-322), we have to use lexical means. For example, *started/began broadcasting*—for the beginning; and *stopped/ceased broadcasting*—for the end. The same can be said about the two external stages. The preparatory stage can be expressed grammatically (i.e., with the help of the prospective marker *going to*: *KSCI-TV is going to broadcast news and entertainment programming in several Asian languages*) or lexically (i.e., with the help of a verb having a similar prospective meaning, e.g., *KSCI-TV intends to broadcast news and entertainment programming in several Asian languages*), but never with *broadcast* only. As for the resultative stage ensuing upon the cessation of the BROADCASTING event, it has to be explicitly mentioned (because broadcasting is not a limitative action whose termination always results in one and the same state). For example, *KSCI-TV in Los Angeles ceased broadcasting news and entertainment programming in Asian languages and, as a result of this, there is currently not a single TV station in L.A. broadcasting in Asian languages*. Or, *KSCI-TV was replaced by another TV station broadcasting in Asian languages*.

In the case of *upload*, the focus is on the terminal and the resultative stages. Indeed, if uploading is an action which is begun in order to be finished, the central stage of the UPLOADING event is neither the beginning (I started to upload a video) nor the middle stage (the moment when my computer is in the process of uploading), but the successful completion (the moment when my computer finishes uploading) as well as the result (the video is available on the Internet). Like the middle stage in *broadcast*, the terminal and the resultative stages in *upload* represent the verb's default aspectual meaning which can be expressed with *upload* only:

> WINK includes areas for poets, fiction writers, journalists, scriptwriters, writers of young adult materials, and so forth. We **upload** drafts of stories and articles and offer critiques. We compare notes on editors, agents, and publishers. (Corpus of Contemporary American English)

It is clear that the underlined *upload* refers to the successful completion of the UPLOADING event: *We upload drafts of stories and articles* = *we upload them until they are uploaded*. As for the resultative stage, it does not need to be mentioned at all because uploading is a telic action whose successful completion always results in one and the same state—the availability of an uploaded entity at the place to which it was uploaded. For example, if I upload a video on YouTube, the result of this can only be the availability of the uploaded video on the YouTube platform.

Other stages, however, cannot be expressed with *upload* only. As with *broadcast*, the preparatory stage requires the prospective marker *going to* or a verb having a similar prospective meaning (e.g., *intend*). Likewise, the beginning requires a verb encoding an inceptive meaning (e.g., *begin/start*). As for the middle stage, it can be expressed both lexically (*I was in the process of uploading a video*) and grammatically, i.e., using the progressive form *I was uploading a video*.

Finally, as regards quantitative aspectuality (Maslov 1973: 403), events can be classified into the following types: (1) single events (e.g., I uploaded a single video on YouTube); (2) multiple events (e.g., I uploaded a number of videos on YouTube); and (3) uninterrupted events which are constantly taking place (e.g., station A broadcasts on frequency X). As for multiple events, they can be further classified into habitual and non-habitual events. Habitual events are regularly-repeating events. For example, it is very likely that the event described by the sentence *KSCI-TV in Los Angeles broadcasts news and entertainment programming in several Asian languages* occurs on a (more or less) regular basis—KSCI-TV **regularly** (e.g., every day at 7 p.m.) broadcasts news and entertainment programs in various Asian languages—and can therefore be considered a habitual event, whereas *I uploaded a number of videos on YouTube* allows both a habitual and a non-habitual interpretation: (1) between 2006-2009 I was regularly uploading some of my videos on YouTube; and (2) between 2006-2009 I was occasionally uploading some of my videos on YouTube.

With respect to quantitative aspectuality, the most important difference between traditional TV broadcasting and uploading videos on YouTube is that the former is an event that is either constantly taking place (station A broadcasts on frequency X) or a habitual, regularly-repeating event (station A broadcasts on frequency X every day between 6 a.m. and 12 p.m.), whereas the latter is usually a non-habitual event (most YouTube users occasionally upload videos on their channel pages). Indeed, in the prototypical case, a traditional TV channel like CNN or ABC is either always on the air or is regularly broadcasting its programs at a particular interval of time. An important manifestation of the habitual character of TV broadcasting is the TV schedule which informs when a TV station is going to broadcast a particular program.

Conversely, uploading a video on YouTube (1) cannot be an uninterrupted event because uploading is a limitative action which exhausts itself as soon as an uploaded entity becomes available at the place to which it was uploaded; and (2) it also can hardly be a habitual event since it is extremely unlikely that YouTube users update their channels with new videos as regularly as traditional TV channels produce and broadcast new programs.

At first glance, this remark may seem to be at odds with what we said about the possibility of a habitual interpretation of *I uploaded a number of videos on YouTube*. That is, in the structure of the UPLOADING event, there is nothing inherently non-habitual, nothing preventing it from being a regularly-repeating event. And, as a matter of fact, a number of YouTube users do indeed (more or less) regularly update their YouTube channels with new videos. Consider, for instance, the below description of Gaijin Navi, a series about foreigner-friendly places in Tokyo made by the YouTube user Stuart Rowe:

> Welcome to Gaijin Navi
> Where **each 2nd friday** we will take you to a different Gaijin friendly part of Tokyo. We'll show you first hand the best places to eat, shop and most importantly DRINK!
> http://www.youtube.com/user/gaijinnavi

Particularly interesting here is that the channel owner (who describes himself as a 24-old teacher of English who lives and works in Japan) promises to add a new video "each 2nd Friday." Given this promise, it can be conjectured that uploading a video on YouTube is perceived by Stuart as a habitual action—an action which, like brushing teeth, has to be repeated after a certain period of time. By why is this actually so?

A possible answer to this question is the television metaphor in which (1) a YouTube channel is analogized to a traditional TV channel; and (2) a video uploaded on YouTube—to a TV program broadcast by a TV channel. As an illustration of this, consider the below forum post in which Stuart refers to Gaijin Navi as a *show*:

> Hello everyone,
> I have started filming a **show** for Gaijin that is shown on the Youtube network.
> (Its not perfect, but we try.)
> Each friday we go to a different part of Tokyo / Saitama / Chiba. And feature a place that is not very well known, and that Gaijin usually dont get to see.
> http://www.jref.com/forum/showthread.php?t=34501

The point here is that if Gaijin Navi is a *show*—the word which in American English can be used to refer to any kind of TV broadcast (Oxford English Dictionary)—then it is supposed to be a habitual, regularly-repeating event. Indeed, if "If it's Sunday, it's Meet the Press," why can it not be "If it's Friday, it's Gaijin Navi"? In other words, Stuart's promise to add a new episode of the show "each 2nd Friday" can be seen as a mapping of the corresponding knowledge about the source domain TRADITIONAL TV CHANNEL—i.e., that TV programs are regularly-repeating events—onto the target domain YOUTUBE CHANNEL.

But despite this example, I insist on the claim that uploading a video on YouTube can only be a non-habitual event. Especially, as far as laymen users like

Stuart Rowe are concerned. To prove this, let us consider the Gaijin Navi's "Videos" section:

Screenshot 22. Gaijin Navi videos

Despite Stuart's promise to add a new video each second Friday, Gaijin Navi contains only eight videos, the last of which was uploaded more than a year ago. As a first approximation, it can be hypothesized that the reason for this is Stuart's busyness at work which is explicitly mentioned in the description of the channel:

> (I have been really busy at work atm, cause of the years closing, but im on holidays now so i should be able to make some new vids soon, got suggestions, pm me. stu 21/12/07
> http://www.youtube.com/user/gaijinnavi

However, according to Stuart, this information was posted on December 21, 2007 and refers to the last days of the year 2007: *I have been really busy at work atm, cause of the years closing*, which implies that Gaijin Navi will be continued in 2008. And, indeed, the last episode of the show was uploaded on January 03, 2008.

Of course, it is possible that Stuart is still very busy at work and therefore does not have enough time for the series. But this is at odds with his description of the job of an English teacher in Japan:

> Hi everyone, Im Stu, I live and work in Japan as an English Teacher, its the easiest job in the world (except if you work for Nova, because now you would be unemployed) But honestly I get paid alot of money to do very little work, thats how I have time to make this series.
> http://www.youtube.com/user/gaijinnavi

Anyway, even if Stuart is indeed very busy at work at the moment, there still arises the question of why he has not removed the promise to update the channel with a new episode of Gaijin Navi each second Friday: How can it be that the last episode was uploaded more than a year ago, but the description of the channel still contains the text *Welcome to Gaijin Navi Where each 2nd friday we will take you to a different Gaijin friendly part of Tokyo*?

The most trivial explanation would be that Stuart ceased to maintain the channel and forgot to remove this information when visiting the channel last time. But according to the "Last Sign in" section, Stuart signed in to his channel last time a month ago (i.e., on February 10, 2009). Why didn't he then remove the no-longer-accurate "programming schedule"?

The answer to this question is the non-habitual character of the event of updating a YouTube channel. That is, there is absolutely no reason why Stuart should necessarily add a new video each second Friday. Why not on Saturday, Monday or on any other day of the week? Why not upload one video on Friday and the other one on Tuesday in two weeks? Why not upload two videos at once and then take a three-week pause? And finally, is it really Stuart's responsibility to inform us about foreigner-friendly places in Japan?!

To conclude, if it makes no difference whether a new video is uploaded each second Friday or on any other day of the week (or even not uploaded at all), then it also makes no difference whether the description of the channel contains this information or not. Thus, it is extremely unlikely that the visitors of Stuart's channel (including those who sincerely like his videos and look forward to seeing new episodes of Gaijin Navi) do actually care whether Stuart keeps his promise of adding a new video each second Friday. Of course, they may regret that Stuart has not uploaded a single video since January 2008, but they may not reproach him for not keeping the promise, for, as just said, Stuart is not responsible for making these videos.

The non-habitual character of the event of uploading a video on YouTube will become even more obvious when we consider a YouTube channel of a user who does not think of in terms of the television metaphor, i.e., the name of the channel does not contain *TV*; and the description does not contain TV-related terms such as *program*, *series*, *show*, etc. For example, the channel of the user tmoney9980 (youtube.com/user/tmoney9980) which was launched on July 14, 2006 contains only 10 videos, all of which were uploaded a year ago. Similarly, the user titetie (youtube.com/user/titetie) launched his channel in March 2006 but, by March 2009, had uploaded only 9 videos. What is more, there are channels without videos. For example, shmoore2's channel (youtube.com/user/shmoore2) has been empty since October 11, 2006—the day when it was launched.

In addition to the non-obligatoriness of posting videos on YouTube, the non-habitual character of this event can also be explained using discourse analysis (DA). Thus from the DA perspective, each of the eight Gaijin Navi episodes can be considered a story about a particular place in Tokyo which Stuart finds interesting from the point of a view of a foreigner residing in Japan. The impression that Stuart's videos are stories arises because they fulfill the *contradiction*-requirement discussed in, e.g., Kraft et al. (1977: 301). That is, a sequence of sentences becomes a story only if it describes an event characterized by *Widerspruch zwischen Plan und Realität* (contradiction between plan and reality), i.e., an event in which something went wrong, not as it was planned. Only "contradictory" events such as, e.g., a traffic accident qualify as *erzählenswert* (worth telling) because they are much more interesting than "non-contradictory" events. For example, a story about driving a car from Cologne to Düsseldorf will be an incredibly boring story if it does not involve a traffic accident or any other "contradictory" event.

As for Gaijin Navi videos, their "contradictory" character is particularly obvious in the above cited description of the channel *Welcome to Gaijin Navi where each second Friday we will take you to a different **Gaijin friendly** part of Tokyo*. As this description makes clear, Stuart's videos are devoted to unusual places, places different from the majority of other places in Tokyo with regard to their foreigner-friendliness. These places are not places which are located on every street corner. Hence, the event of finding these places cannot be a habitual, regularly-repeating event. For events repeating on a regular basis (e.g., each second Friday) do not fulfill the *contradiction*-requirement and therefore cannot be perceived as unusual.

This is a very important finding which seems to be true of all videos that have ever been uploaded on the YouTube platform. For as in the case of story-telling or even speaking in general, the main motivation for uploading a video on YouTube is the wish to achieve success, i.e., attract the maximum number of viewers and receive positive comments and ratings. (The idea that we speak in order to achieve success (i.e., produce an impression on other people) was originally expressed by the American psycholinguist George Zipf (1949: 19); cf. Keller and Kirschbaum (2003: 12).) Accordingly, if the achievement of success is the primary motivation for using the YouTube platform, then all videos posted there must fulfill the *contradiction*-requirement (i.e., show something unusual). But as illustrated by the Stuart example, events fulfilling the *contradiction*-requirement—events which, due to their unusual character, are perceived as interesting and worth telling—can only have a non-habitual aspectual meaning, i.e., be rarely-occurring events rather than habitual events repeating "each second Friday."

To conclude: We have established that uploading a video on YouTube and traditional TV broadcasting are events that exhibit considerable aspectual differences. As for qualitative aspectuality, the former is a limitative action which exhausts itself as soon as videos uploaded by YouTube users become available on their channel pages. Broadcasting is, by contrast, a non-limitative action which is begun not in order to be finished. As for linear aspectuality, uploading is an event of a terminative Aktionsart in which the focus is on the terminal stage—the successful completion of the UPLOADING event resulting in the availability of the uploaded video at the place to which it was uploaded—whereas *broadcast* has a durative Aktionsart which emphasizes the middle stage (or duration) of the BROADCASTING event. Finally, with regard to quantitative aspectuality, the difference is that traditional TV broadcasting is either an event that always takes place (station A always broadcasts on frequency X) or is a habitual event repeating on a regular basis (station A broadcasts every day between 6 a.m. and 12 p.m.), whereas uploading a video on YouTube is a non-habitual, irregularly-occurring event.

9.2.2. Why *broadcast* and *channel*?

Given these differences, let us now proceed to the origin of the mapping "broadcast → upload." How can uploading a video on YouTube be analogized to traditional TV broadcasting?

The answer to this question is most likely the well-known metonymy ACTION FOR RESULT. The point here is that in *broadcast yourself* (screenshot 20), *broadcast* does not really mean "start uploading videos on your YouTube channel" (which was taken for granted in the previous discussion), but refers to the result of this action—the availability of uploaded videos on the YouTube platform. For example, one of Britney Spears' hits "Born To Make You Happy" is available at youtube.com/watch?v=DpiD4zVJE7A, i.e., any time you visit the page, YouTube will be playing this clip for you. This is the essence of "broadcasting" on YouTube. And if we compare it with traditional TV broadcasting, we will see that the former does not differ from the latter with regard to Aktionsarten.

Let us start with quantitative aspectuality. As said above, traditional TV broadcasting is usually an event that always takes place, i.e., traditional TV channels like CNN or BBC are usually always on the air broadcasting films, programs, commercials, etc. Likewise, YouTube channels and videos uploaded on them are always available on the Internet and therefore, like traditional TV channels, can "broadcast" all the time, i.e., be always played and watched by at least one YouTube user. (Whether this takes place or not depends entirely on users' interest to a particular video or a channel.) Accordingly, if YouTube broadcasting is an event that always takes place, it can only be a non-limitative event which is begun not in order to be finished. That is, YouTube users upload videos on their channel pages not in order to remove them once they achieve success but to "broadcast" them as long as YouTube exists. Finally, given the non-limitative character of YouTube broadcasting, it is also clear that the most important stage of this event is not the beginning (the moment when the channel owner is uploading a video) nor the end (the moment when s/he is removing it), but the middle stage—the moment when the video is uploaded on YouTube so that other users can watch it anytime they want.

Taking this into account, we can now conclude that YouTube broadcasting does not differ from traditional TV broadcasting with respect to Aktionsarten. This explains why *broadcast* can be used in the context of a YouTube channel without resulting in a semantic anomaly.

Also, it can be suggested that aspectual similarities between traditional TV broadcasting and broadcasting on YouTube is the only reason why a YouTube channel was metaphorized as a traditional TV channel. Indeed, in what other respects is the former similar to the latter?

Many would perhaps argue that both a YouTube channel and a TV channel broadcast **videos**. (This can be considered the experiential similarity between the former and the latter.) But a YouTube channel seems to be much better analogizable to an archive of videos (which were posted at different times and are now available at a particular location on the Internet) rather than to a TV channel live-streaming videos. So, why have the creators chosen the signifier *channel*?

The answers to this question are (1) the original intensional semantics of *archive*; and again (2) aspectual similarities between TV broadcasting and broadcasting on YouTube. As for the former, consider, first of all, the definition of an *archive* as "a place or collection containing records, documents, or other materials of historical interest" (American Heritage Dictionary). As mentioned in chapter 2, the Internet is, in stark contrast to a traditional archive, an archive of non-selected information (Jampolski 1998: 252) which abounds in things (e.g., pornography) which we usually do not find in traditional archives. Another important difference is that in the real-world only few people have physical access to archives (i.e., to buildings containing documents and materials of historical interest), whereas the Internet is geared to be used by the maximum number of people (ibid. p. 241).

This characterization neatly applies to YouTube videos which (1) are uploaded in order to be watched, rated, and commented on by the maximum number of other users; and (2) for this purpose, can be freely accessed by anyone whose computer is connected to the Internet.

Of course, it can be argued that this difference does not prevent us from using the term *archive* referring to Internet archives. Thus the global computer network has a number of Web sites describing themselves as archives. Consider, for example, the famous arXiv.org, an archive of preprints of articles in Physics, Mathematics, Computer Sciences, and disciplines alike. Similar to traditional archives, arXiv.org represents a collection of materials which can be said to be of historical interest for the development of these disciplines. But unlike traditional archives, arXiv.org is an Open Access archive, i.e., a Web site which can be freely accessed by all Internet users (i.e., all Web users including those who are not physicists, mathematicians, computer scientists, etc., can access preprints of articles stored in arXiv.org). Accordingly, the Open Access nature of an Internet archive is not a hindrance for the use of *archive* in the context of a Web site like arXiv.org.

Nevertheless, many Internet archives resemble traditional archives in that they contain materials intended to be used by a relatively small number of people. For example, Online Archive of California (a database of manuscripts of images from institutions across California), Archive of European Integration (electronic repository of research materials on the topic of European integration), Digital Archive of European Architecture (archive of images of architecture from around the world), National Archive of Criminal Justice Data, etc. It is clear that users who are not researchers working in these fields will most likely never visit these archives. (So, it turns out that Open Access understood as access for everyone is, strictly speaking, superfluous: Users who are not professionally interested in Physics, Mathematics, Computer Sciences, etc., do not really need an Open Access to preprints of articles in these disciplines stored in arXiv.org.) And although the same can be said about some YouTube channels—for example, if you are not interested in foreigner-friendly places in Tokyo, you will perhaps never visit Stuart's Gaijin Navi channel—it is clear that the average YouTube channel maintained by an amateur video-maker like Stuart Rowe can attract the attention of a much larger audience than arXiv.org or Archive of European Architecture.

But the main reason for the creators' choice of *channel* are the aspectual similarities between a YouTube channel and a traditional TV channel. As we have established, YouTube broadcasting is similar to TV broadcasting with regard to all kinds of aspectual meanings: Both the former and the latter are events that always take place (quantitative aspectuality). Both the former and the latter are non-limitative events which are begun not in order to be finished (qualitative aspectuality). And both the former and the latter are durative events whose duration (or the middle stage) is much more important than the beginning and the end (linear aspectuality).

But what about an archive? In contrast to *channel*, *archive* seems to have no aspectual meaning at all. Thus, whereas the word *channel*, despite being a noun, is more like a verb in that it signifies a concept which includes a number of dynamic situations—broadcasting, production of programs, etc.—*archive* is a prototypical noun whose semantic content seems to be fully captured by the above definition *place or collection containing records, documents or other materials*. A traditional archive is indeed nothing more than a place (or collection) containing such materials. Particularly important here is that there seem to be no (or very few) dynamic situations in which these materials are involved. For example, videos lying on shelves in TV channels' archives are usually not used for anything else apart from being physically present in those archives (or, in other words, apart from lying on a shelf). These videos are usually not used for broadcasting since the prototypical TV channel usually broadcasts new videos (which, however, may from time to time contain old videos: consider, for example, the so-called "Best of___" editions of a particular program consisting of the program's already broadcast selected videos).

Summarizing: If something (a video or a print document) is added to an archive, it will be used again only on some rare occasions when there is a special reason to use it. During the rest of the time, however, it will be involved in no dynamic situations. The only event in which it will be involved will be being physically present in an archive (i.e., lying on a shelf). But this is hardly a dynamic event: there is no "dynamics" in that something is on a shelf, especially if the thing in question is an inanimate entity which cannot put itself on a shelf on its own.

This is the "logic" of a traditional archive which, as we have seen, to a very large extent, also applies to Internet archives like arXiv.org or Archive of European Architecture: These contain materials which are used by a relatively small number of users on very few occasions. But the "logic" of a YouTube channel is a different one. A YouTube channel is not an archive in which videos are "lying on a shelf," but a channel which "broadcasts" them to channel visitors.

9.2.3. Subscribers

Finally, let us briefly discuss another important element of a YouTube channel: the "Subscribers" section. The question which will be dealt with in the remainder of this section is whether "Subscribers" represents one of the ontological mappings of the conceptual metaphor A YOUTUBE CHANNEL IS A TRADITIONAL TV CHANNEL.

This question arises because in real-life the concept of a subscriber is an important element of the domain PAY TELEVISION. (That is, to be able to view a Pay-TV channel, we have to subscribe to it.)

In light of what was said above, the answer to this question seems to be no. First of all, because subscribing to a YouTube channel differs from subscribing to a Pay-TV channel in many essential respects. Among other things, in the case of YouTube channels, we don't have to pay money to their owners in order to be able to subscribe to them: Like arXiv.org, these are Open Access archives which can be accessed by anyone whose computer is connected to the Internet.

Second, traditional Pay-TV channels do not have the "Subscribers" section. They do keep records of their subscribers, but, unlike YouTube channels (see screenshot 23), they do not make this information publicly available:

Screenshot 23. "Subscribers" section on a YouTube channel

But the most important argument against attributing the presence of "Subscribers" to the television metaphor is the fact that "Subscribers" is one of the key features of what we call the *Web 2.0 era*. That is, a number of 2.0 Web sites whose owners do not think of them in terms of the television metaphor have "Subscribers." For example, on SNS Web sites users can subscribe to their friends' profiles. On Flickr—to other users' photostreams. On Delicious—to other users' bookmarks. Also, the majority of Web sites which have existed since the early years of the Internet (e.g., Web sites of traditional print and electronic media) can nowadays be subscribed to by means of RSS.

But the situation is not that easy as it may seem at first glance. The problem here is that YouTube channels can be subscribed to in two different ways. First of all, as a registered user you can go to a channel page you wish to subscribe to and click on "Subscribe," as shown on screenshot 24. But if you don't have a YouTube account, you can nevertheless subscribe to any YouTube channel by creating an RSS feed for it. (I mentioned this in the previous chapter.)

That YouTube allows users to subscribe to channels by means of RSS is understandable: As mentioned in the previous chapter, this is nowadays the standard, the genuinely Web 2.0 way of subscribing on the Internet. By what about

Screenshot 24. Subscribing to Britney Spears' YouTube channel

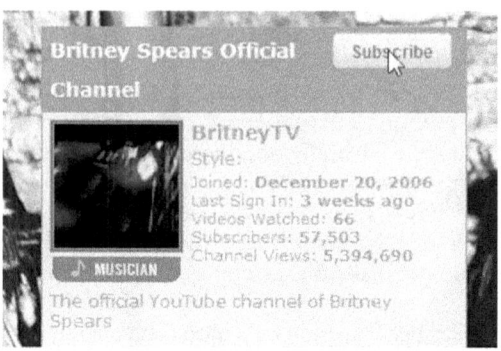

the non-RSS-based subscription?

It is possible that its co-existence with RSS is due to the conceptual metaphor A YOUTUBE CHANNEL IS A TRADITIONAL TV CHANNEL. Thus, despite the previously named differences between subscribing to a YouTube channel and subscribing in the real-world, "Subscribers" represents an ontological mapping of the source domain TRADITIONAL TV CHANNEL onto the target domain YOUTUBE CHANNEL. That is, YouTube creators transferred the concept of a subscriber from the former onto the latter when designing YouTube channels. The reason for this may be the fact that as in real-life, "Subscribers" can serve as an indicator of a channel's success (and as we said, the achievement of success is the primary motivation for launching a YouTube channel): The more subscribers it has, the more successful is the channel owner, the more successful are the videos which s/he uploaded.

Also, it must be noted that on YouTube a subscriber (who has a YouTube account) is simultaneously a channel owner her/himself. Accordingly, subscribing to a YouTube channel is very often an attempt to attract the channel owner's attention to the subscriber's own channel. Thus if I subscribe to Stuart Rowe's Gaijin Navi show by creating an RSS feed for his YouTube channel, he will never learn about the fact of my subscription because subscribing to an RSS feed is anonymous. However, if I subscribe to his channel using my own YouTube channel, he will be aware of this fact since my username will then appear in his channel's "Subscribers" section. Given these facts, it must be now clear why YouTube allows users to subscribe to other users' channels in two different ways. Those who want to stay anonymous can subscribe using RSS. Those who want to promote their own videos can subscribe using their own YouTube channels.

9.3. Intension

At the end of the chapter, let us turn our attention to the conceptual meaning of *channel*. As in the previous case studies, the question that will be addressed below is whether language users are consciously aware of (at least some of) the differences between a YouTube channel and a traditional TV channel which were discussed in the previous sections.

As for the creators' perspective, I have already implicitly answered this question citing the YouTube FAQ and Help Center definitions of *channel* (see p. 111). The fact that *channel* is defined as *profile page, user's page,* and *centralized location* clearly indicates that *a YouTube channel* is a lexeme different from *a traditional TV channel.* (The same is true of users. As will be shown below, linguistically, this is reflected in the fact that it is only a YouTube channel (but not a traditional TV channel) which can be analogized to such concepts as, e.g., HOMEPAGE, SNS PROFILE PAGE, ARCHIVE, etc.)

As for the channel owners' perspective, the most interesting question is whether they have accepted the television metaphor proposed by the creators. Do they really metaphorize YouTube channels as TV channels? Or is *channel* a term of zero metaphoricity; the term which they use simply because they are "forced" to use it by the creators?

This question needs to be considered because, as was stated in chapter 2, metaphorical expressions which do not fulfill the additional naming requirement tend to lose their original metaphoricity and eventually develop into homonyms of their source concepts. But this does not seem to be true of *channel*. The television metaphor is still alive, for even in August 2008 a number of newly-launched YouTube channels were called *TVs*. Consider, for example, Boulder-GangTV,[5] a channel that was launched on August 03, 2008 by the user Robert from Tunbridge Wells, U.K. That *TV* is still used as a constituent of the name of a YouTube channel is the best empirical evidence for the claim that A YOUTUBE CHANNEL IS A TV CHANNEL, as understood by (at least some active) users of the YouTube platform.

At the same time, it is important to emphasize that A YOUTUBE CHANNEL IS NOT ONLY A TV CHANNEL. That is, in addition to being a TV CHANNEL, the target domain YOUTUBE CHANNEL is also understood in terms of several other source domains. For example, in terms of an SNS PROFILE PAGE and a TRADITIONAL HOMEPAGE:

> This is **my homepage on Youtube.com** Youtube.com/user/NoiseSonicBoom Always Subscribe and become friends with me. Invites are always accepted [...]
> http://www.youtube.com/watch?v=Kx_YzPQdBoE

---

[5] http://www.youtube.com/user/BoulderGangTV

That *homepage* can be used as a synonym of *channel* is because of the experiential similarity between YouTube channels and traditional homepages. Like SNS profiles, YouTube channels can, and as a matter of fact, are often used as homepages (e.g., celebrity channels).

As for the SNS profile page metaphor, consider the below quotes:

> 8hands - Browse all **social networking website[s]** MySpace, FaceBook, **YouTube**, Flickr and Twitter at once. Welcome to the multitasking master program for all ...
> http://tinyurl.com/ckjgng

> A social network aggregator simply links and/or shows your profiles from other **social networks** (i.e. Myspace, Friendster, Facebook, **Youtube**). ...
> http://www.otherego.com/

As you can see, in them, YouTube is referred to as a *social networking Web site* (even though, in terms of genres, this is not true: YouTube is not an SNS, but a video-sharing service). As stated in the beginning of the chapter, the reason for this is that a YouTube channel contains FRIENDS2 (i.e., allows channel owners to "friend" and be "friended" by other users) and therefore fulfills the main SNS-hood requirement.

Finally, a YouTube channel is also metaphorized as an archive, a collection, and a repository of videos:

> P.S. check out **my youtube archive** http://youtube.com/user/zylebenezer
> http://zyllable.wordpress.com/2008/07/24/bakdat/

> Hello! Welcome **to my collection of videos on YouTube**.
> http://www.youtube.com/user/ZackScott

> **My YouTube repository** for http://trev.id.au/
> http://www.youtube.com/user/trevidau

In connection with these examples (which may seem to question the plausibility of our observations about the aspectual differences between an archive and a channel), it must be stressed that by arguing that a YouTube channel is not an archive because a video added to an archive is usually not used for broadcasting, I did not mean that a YouTube channel cannot be analogized to an archive. What I meant was that the aspectual differences between a YouTube channel and an archive could have been the main reason for the creators' choice of the word *channel* instead of *archive*, *repository*, *collection*, or any other similar expression: If a YouTube channel had been called an *archive*, the YouTube platform would not be the most popular video-sharing Web site. For the term *channel* connotes activity—constant production of new videos and broadcasting—and is therefore capable of attracting much larger audiences than the more "passive" *archive*. As an illustration of this, consider the replacement of *TV* in the names of YouTube channels such as, e.g., BritneyTV and BoulderGangTV, by *archive*. In both cases, the result is the change of connotation: both BritneyArchive and BoulderGangArchive connote passivity on the part of the Archive owners, i.e., that neither Britney Spears nor the user Robert update their archives with new videos. But, as just said, all this does not mean that ARCHIVE cannot serve as an alternative source domain for the target domain YOUTUBE CHANNEL co-existing with TV channel, homepage and SNS profile page metaphors.

10. Concluding remarks

In this study, we have attempted to semantically decompose some of the metaphorical expressions associated with two particular Web 2.0 practices: social networking Web sites and folksonomies. The expressions under consideration were analyzed from the point of view of both the extensional and the intensional approaches to meaning, i.e., the purpose of the study was to find out both what these expressions stand for (extensional/referential approach) and what they mean (intensional/conceptual approach).

We have established that the semantic development undergone by these expressions can be classified into two categories: (1) change of extensional meaning which has not resulted in change of intensional meaning; and (2) change of extensional meaning accompanied by change of intensional meaning.

As for the former category, our central finding is that intensional meaning does not change when referential changes do not affect the core elements (or actants) of events denoted by these expressions. For example, *sign up* (in *sign up for Facebook*), *subscribe* (in *subscribe to an RSS feed*), SuperFive "kiss," etc., mean what they literally stand for, even though (1) the event SIGNING UP FOR FACEBOOK does not involve "admission offices"; (2) the event SUBSCRIBING TO AN RSS FEED does not involve "subscription fees"; and (3) the event SUPER-FIVING WITH THE "KISS" does not involve physical kissing. The reason for this is that all these differences concern the non-core element (or circumstant of) Manner specifying how these actions are performed in real-life and on the Internet. (E.g., in real-life we kiss *by physically kissing each other*; on hi5—*by sending the recipient the SuperFive "kiss."*) In contrast, *immatrikulieren* (in *im StudiVZ immatrikulieren*) does not mean "matriculate" because StudiVZ is not a university (i.e., one of the core elements/actants of the MATRICULATION event), but only an online SNS designed to be used by university students.

In addition to this, change of intensional meaning can be brought about by the re-conceptualization of the original concept. For example, (1) *profile* (in the context of an SNS profile page) came to be re-conceptualized as a personal Web site; (2) *friend* (in the context of an SNS friend)—as a subscriber to the content generated by the profile owner; (3) social bookmarking services—as search engines; (4) subscribing to an RSS feed—as bookmarking a Web page, (5) YouTube channels—as SNS profile pages, etc.

I hope, this study will not be the last word on the topic of Web 2.0 metaphors, but will instead spark off the researchers' interest to such issues as, e.g., the socio-linguistics of Web 2.0 metaphors: That is, for example, who are those users who re-conceptualized social networking services as Web hosting services, SNS member profiles as personal Web sites, SNS friends as subscribers?

Apart from this, a similar semantic analysis can be applied to other Web 2.0 services. What is, for example, the difference between SNS profile pages and blog pages? At first glance, this may seem a rather trivial question. They differ with regard to genre: The former are SNS profile pages, the latter are blog pages. But the situation is not that easy since almost everything we know about SNS profile pages can also be said about blog pages. First of all, like an SNS profile page, a blog page can be used as a homepage: As, e.g., O'Reilly (2005: online) points out, "[a]t its most basic, a blog is just a personal home page in diary format." Accordingly, like SNSs, blogging services can also be seen as a Web 2.0 alternative to classical personal Web sites. Also, bloggers can add each other as friends (i.e., use blog as an SNS). Like an SNS profile page, a blog page contains what can be considered a $PROFILE2\_1.0$-like description of the blog owner. And so on.

The situation with blog pages is similar to YouTube channel pages which, in addition to being channel pages, can be metaphorized as SNS profile pages. But there is an important difference: In the case of YouTube channels, the SNS profile page metaphor represents a secondary metaphorical conception of a YouTube channel. That is, A YOUTUBE CHANNEL is, first of all, A TRADITIONAL TV CHANNEL and only then AN SNS PROFILE PAGE, A PERSONAL WEB SITE, AN ARCHIVE, etc. But what is the primary metaphorical conception of a blog page? Is it really a logbook—i.e., "a record book with periodic entries" (American Heritage Dictionary)—as the English term *blog* (the blend of *Web* and *log*) seems to suggest? If yes, in what respects are traditional logbooks different from Web logs? Which entities and which of our knowledge about the source domain LOGBOOK have correspondences in the target domain WEB LOG?

I hope that these and other similar issues will be extensively dealt with in future studies devoted to Web 2.0 metaphors as well as to Web 2.0 in general.

References

American Heritage Dictionary of the English Language. 2000. Fourth edition. http://www.bartleby.com/61/.

Apresjan, Yuri D. 1974. Regular Polysemy. *Linguistics* 142, 5-32.

Barbatsis, Gretchen, Fegan, Michael, and Kenneth Hansen 1999. The Performance of Cyberspace: An Exploration into Computer-Mediated Reality. *Journal of Computer-Mediated Communication* 5 (1) http://jcmc.indiana.edu/vol5/issue1/barbatsis.html.

Barlow, John Perry 1996. A Declaration of the Independence of Cyberspace. http://homes.eff.org/~barlow/Declaration-Final.html.

Baumgärtel, Tilman 1998. Das Internet als imaginäres Museum. http://duplox.wzb.eu/texte/tb/.

Beer, David 2008. Social Network(ing) Sites...Revisiting the Story So Far: A Response to Danah Boyd & Nicole Ellison. *Journal of Computer-Mediated Communication* 13 (2), 516-529.

Blank, Andreas 1997. *Prinzipien des lexikalischen Bedeutungswandels am Beispiel der romanischen Sprachen*. Tübingen: Niemeyer.

Blavin, Jonathan H. and I. Glenn Cohen 2002. Gore, Gibson, and Goldsmith: The Evolution of Internet Metaphors in Law and Commentary. *Harvard Journal of Law and Technology* 16 (1), 265-285.

Bloomfield, Leonard. 1933. *Language*. New York: Henry Holt and Co.

boyd, Danah M. and Nicole B. Ellison 2007. Social Network Sites: Definition, History, and Scholarship. *Journal of Computer-Mediated Communication* 13 (1) http://jcmc.indiana.edu/vol13/issue1/boyd.ellison.html.

British National Corpus. http://corpus.byu.edu/bnc/.

Cambridge Dictionary of American English. 2008. Second edition. http://dictionary.cambridge.org/Default.asp?dict=A.

Canzler, Weert, Helmers, Sabine, and Ute Hoffmann 1997. Die Datenautobahn: Sinn und Unsinn einer populären Metapher. In: Dierkes, Meinolf (ed.) Technikgenese. Befunde aus einem Forschungsprogramm. Berlin: Ed. Sigma, pp. 167-192.

Cohen, Julie E. 2007. Cyberspace as/and Space. *Columbia Law Review* 107, 210-256.

Compact Oxford English Dictionary of Current English. 2005. Third edition. http://www.oup.com/uk/catalogue/?ci=9780198610229&view=ask.

Corpus of Contemporary American English. http://www.americancorpus.org/.

Cruse, Alan 2004. *Meaning in Language. An Introduction to Semantics and Pragmatics*. Second Edition. Oxford et al.: Oxford University Press.

Deignan, Alice 2005. *Metaphor and Corpus Linguistics*. Amsterdam; Philadelphia: John Benjamins Publishing Company.

Dobrovol'skij, Dmitrij O. 1997. *Idiome im mentalen Lexikon. Ziele und Methoden der kognitivbasierten Phraseologieforschung*. Trier: WVT.

___and Elisabeth Piirainen 2005. *Figurative Language. Cross-Cultural and Cross-Linguistic Perspective*. Amsterdam et al.: Elsevier.

Döring, Nicola 2002. Personal Home Pages on the Web. A Review of Research. *Journal of Computer-Mediated Communication* 7 (3) http://jcmc.indiana.edu/vol7/issue3/doering.html.

Ellison, Nicole B., Steinfield, Charles, and Cliff Lampe 2007. The Benefits of Facebook "Friends:" Social Capital and College Students' Use of Online Social Network Sites. *Journal of Computer-Mediated Communication* 12 (4) http://jcmc.indiana.edu/vol12/issue4/ellison.html.

FrameNet. http://framenet.icsi.berkeley.edu/.

Frawley, William 1992. *Linguistic Semantics*. Hilsdale, NJ: Erlbaum.

Gehring, Eva 2004. *Medienmetaphorik: Das Internet im Fokus seiner räumlichen Metaphorik*. Berlin: dissertation.de.

Gozzi, Raymond 1994a. The Information Superhighway Metaphor. *ETC.: A Review of General Semantics* 51 (3), 321-327.

___1994b. The Cyberspace Metaphor. *ETC.: A Review of General Semantics* 51 (2), 218-223.

___1997. Metaphors Converging on the Internet. *ETC.: A Review of General Semantics* 54 (4), 479-486.

___2006. Google. *ETC.: A Review of General Semantics* 63 (4), 444-446.

Google News Archive Search. http://news.google.com/archivesearch.

Helmers, Sabine, Hoffmann, Ute, and Jeanette Hofmann 1994. Alles Datenautobahn—oder was? Entwicklungspfade in eine vernetzte Zukunft. http://duplox.wzb.eu/texte/ausblick/.

Herring, Susan C. 2007. A Faceted Classification Scheme for Computer-Mediated Discourse. *Language@Internet* 4 (1) http://www.languageatinternet.de/articles/2007/761/index_html/.

Hill, Russell A. and Robin I. M. Dunbar 2003. Social Network Size in Humans. *Human Nature* 14 (1), 53-72.

Hock, Hans Heinrich 1986. *Principles of Historical Linguistics.* Berlin; New York: Mouton de Gruyter.

Hofmann, Jeanette 1996. Automobil-und Datenverkehr: Ein ernsthaftes Missverhältnis. *Dialog*, 24-25.

Hughes, Geoffrey 1988. *Words in Time: A Social History of the English Vocabulary.* Oxford: Blackwell.

Jamet, Denis 2002. Les métaphores d'Internet—«Comment surfer sur les autoroutes de l'information sans se prendre les pieds dans la corbeille». http://www.metaphorik.de/aufsaetze/jamet-internet.htm.

Jampolski, Michail 1998. Das Internet oder: das postarchivarische Bewusstsein. In: Schmid, Ullrich (ed.), pp. 241-262.

Jansen, Silke 2002. Metaphern im Sprachkontakt—anhand von Beispielen aus dem Französischen und Spanischen Internetwortschatz. *Metaphorik.de* 03, 44-74. http://www.metaphorik.de/03/jansen.htm.

___2005. *Sprachliches Lehngut im World Wide Web*. Tübingen: Gunter Narr Verlag.

Johnson, Mark 2007. *The Meaning of the Body. Aesthetics of Human Understanding*. Chicago: The University of Chicago Press.

Keller, Rudi and Ilja Kirschbaum 2003. *Bedeutungswandel. Eine Einführung*. Berlin; New York: Walter de Gruyter.

Kortmann, Bernd 2005. *English Linguistics: Essentials*. Berlin: Cornelsen.

Kövecses, Zoltán 1995. American Friendship and the Scope of Metaphor. *Cognitive Linguistics* 6 (4), 315-346.

___2000. *Metaphor and Emotion. Language, Culture, and Body in Human Feeling*. Cambridge et al.: Cambridge University Press.

___2002. *Metaphor. A Practical Introduction*. Oxford et al.: Oxford University Press.

___2005. *Metaphor in Culture. Universality and Variation*. Cambridge et al.: Cambridge University Press.

___2006. *Language, Mind, and Culture. A Practical Dictionary*. Oxford et al.: Oxford University Press.

___and Günter Radden 1998. Metonymy: Developing a Cognitive Linguistic View. *Cognitive Linguistics* 9 (1), 37-77.

Kraft, Eberhardt, Kurt, Nikolaus, and Uta Quasthoff 1977. Die Konstitution der konversationellen Erzählung. *Folia Linguistica* 11 (3-4), 287-337.

Lakoff, George 1987. *Women, Fire, and Dangerous Things. What Categories Reveal about the Mind*. Chicago: The University of Chicago Press.

___2008. The Neural Theory of Metaphor. In: Gibbs, Raymond W. (ed.) *The Cambridge Handbook of Metaphor and Thought*. Cambridge et al.: Cambridge University Press, pp. 17-38.

___and Mark Johnson 1980. *Metaphors We Live by*. Chicago: The University of Chicago Press.

___1999. *Philosophy in the Flesh. The Embodied Mind and Its Challenge to Western Thought*. New York: Basic Books.

___and Mark Turner 1989. *More than Cool Reason. A Field Guide to Poetic Metaphor*. Chicago: The University of Chicago Press.

___and Elisabeth Wehling 2008. Auf leisen Sohlen ins Gehirn. Politische Sprache und ihre heimliche Macht. Heidelberg: Carl-Auer-Systeme.

Leise, Fred, Fast, Karl, and Mike Steckel 2002. What is a Controlled Vocabulary? http://www.boxesandarrows.com/view/what_is_a_controlled_vocabulary_.

Lemley, Mark A. 2002. Place and Cyberspace. University of California at Berkeley, School of Public Law and Legal Theory Research Paper No. 102.

Löbner, Sebastian 2002. *Understanding Semantics*. London: Arnold.

Lombard, Carol G. 2005. Conceptual Metaphors in Computer Networking Technology. *Southern African Linguistics and Applied Language Studies* 23 (2), 177-185.

Madsen, Kim Halskov 1994. A Guide to Metaphorical Design. *Communications of the ACM* 37 (12), 57-62.

Maglio, Paul P. and Teenie Matlock 1999. The Conceptual Structure of Information Space. In: Munro, Alan J., Hook, Kristina, and David Benyon (eds.) *Social Navigation of Information Space*. London: Springer, pp. 155-173.

Markham, Annette N. 2003. Metaphors Reflecting and Shaping the Reality of the Internet: Tool, Place, Way of Being. http://markham.internetinquiry.org/writing/MarkhamTPW.pdf.

Maslov, Jurij. 1973. Universal'nye semantičeskie komponenty v soderžanii grammatičeskoj kategorii soveršennogo/nesoveršennogo vida. In: Maslov, Jurij (2004), pp. 396-410.

___1978. K osnovanijam sopostavitel'noj aspektologii. In: Maslov, Jurij (2004), pp. 305-364.

___2004. *Izbrannye trudy. Aspektologija. Obščee jazykoznanie*. Moskva: Jaziki Slavjanskoj Kultury.

Mel'čuk, Igor 1995. Phrasemes in Language and Phraseology in Linguistics. In: Everaert, Martin (ed.) *Idioms: Structural and Psychological Perspectives.* Hilsdale: Lawrence Erlbaum Associates, pp. 167-233.

___2001. *Kurs obščej morfologii. Morfologičeskie znaki.* Moskau; Wien: Wiener Slawistischer Almanach = Mel'čuk, Igor 1997. *Cours de Morphologie Générale. Cinquième Partie: Signes Morphologiques.* Montréal: Les Pr. del' Univ. de Montréal.

___2004. Actants in Semantics and Syntax I: Actants in Semantics. *Linguistics* 42 (1), 1-66.

Merriam-Webster Online. http://www.merriam-webster.com/.

Merriam-Webster Unabridged 2002. Third new international edition. Springfield, Mass.: Merriam-Webster.

Meyer, Ingrid, Zaluski, Victoria, and Kristen Mackintosh 1997. Metaphorical Internet Terms. A Conceptual and Structural Analysis. *Terminology* 4 (1), 1-33.

Mihalache, Adrian 2002. The Cyber Space-Time Continuum: Meaning and Metaphor. *The Information Society* 18 (4), 293-301.

Mika, Peter 2005. Ontologies are US: A Unified Model of Social Networks and Semantics. In: Gil, Yolanda, Motta, Enrico, Benjamins, V. Richard, and Mark A. Musen (eds.) *The Semantic Web—ISWC 2005.* Berlin; Heidelberg: Springer, pp. 522-536.

Nunberg, Geoffrey, Sag, Ivan A., and Thomas Wasow 1994. Idioms. *Language* 70 (3), 491-538.

Núñez, Francesc 2004. Metáforas de Internet. *Revista Digital d'Humanitats* 6, 1-10.

Ogden, Charles K. and Ivor A. Richards 1923. *The Meaning of Meaning.* San Diego: A Harverst/HBJ Book.

O'Reilly, Tim 2005. What is Web 2.0? Design Patterns and Business Models for the Next Generation of Software.
http://www.oreillynet.com/pub/a/oreilly/tim/news/2005/09/30/what-is-web-20.html.

Oxford English Dictionary. 1989. Second edition. Oxford et al.: Oxford University Press.

Palmquist, Ruth A. 1996. The Search for an Internet Metaphor: A Comparison of Literatures.
http://www.asis.org/annual-96/ElectronicProceedings/palmquist.html.

Peters, Isabella and Katrin Weller 2008. Tag Gardening for Folksonomy Enrichment and Maintenance. *Webology* 5 (3)
http://www.webology.ir/2008/v5n3/a58.html.

Plungjan, Vladimir A. 2000. *Obščaja morfologija. Vvedenie v problematiku.* Moskva: Editorial URSS.

Porto Requejo, María Dolores 2007. The Construction of the Concept Internet through Metaphors. *Culture, Language & Representation* 5, 195-207.

Ratzan, Lee 2000. Making Sense of the Web: A Metaphorical Approach. *Information Research* 6 (1)
http://informationr.net/ir/6-1/paper85.html.

Reichertz, Jo 1998. Metaphern als Mittel der Sinnzuschreibung in der 'Computerwelt.' In: Holly, Werner and Ulrich Biere (eds.): *Medien im Wandel.* Opladen: Westdeutscher Verlag, pp. 173-186.

Renkema, Jan 2004. *Introduction to Discourse Studies.* Amsterdam; Philadelphia: John Benjamins Publishing Company.

Rohrer, Tim 1997. Conceptual Blending on the Information Highway: How Metaphorical Inferences Work. In: Liebert, Wolf-Andreas, Redeker, Gisela, and Linda R. Waugh (eds.) *Discourse and Perspective in Cognitive Linguistics.* Amsterdam; Philadelphia: John Benjamins Publishing Company, pp. 185-204.

___2001. Even the Interface is for Sale: Metaphors, Visual Blends and the Hidden Ideology of the Internet. In: Dirven, René, Hawkins, Bruce, and Esra Sandikcioglu (eds.) *Language and Ideology.* Amsterdam; Philadelphia: John Benjamins Publishing Company, pp. 189-214.

Rolf, Eckard 2005. *Metaphertheorien: Typologie, Darstellung, Bibliographie.* Berlin; New York: Walter de Gruyter.

Ruppenhofer, Josef, Ellsworth, Michael, Petruck, Miriam R. L., Johnson, Christopher R., and Jan Scheffczyk 2006. FrameNet II: Extended Theory and Practice. http://framenet.icsi.berkeley.edu/book/book.html#intro.

Schmid, Ullrich (ed.) 2005. *Russische Medientheorien*. Bern: Haupt.

Schnadwinkel, Birte 2002. Neue Medien Neue Metaphern? Sprachliche Erschließung des neuen Mediums Internet durch Metaphern (deutsch-französisch). M.A. thesis, University of Hamburg.

Smilowitz, Elissa D. 1996. Do Metaphors Make Web Browsers Easier to Use? http://www.baddesigns.com/mswebcnf.htm.

Sperber, Hans 1923. *Einführung in die Bedeutungslehre*. Bonn: Kurt Schroeter Verlag.

Stefik, Mark 1996. *Internet Dreams. Archetypes, Myths, and Metaphors*. Cambridge, Mass.: MIT Press.

Sullivan, Karen 2007. Grammar in Metaphor: A Construction Grammar Account of Metaphoric Language. Ph.D. Thesis. University of California at Berkeley.

Taylor, John R. 2002. *Cognitive Grammar*. Oxford et al.: Oxford University Press.

Tomaszewski, Zach 2002. Conceptual Metaphors of the World Wide Web. http://www2.hawaii.edu/~ztomasze/ling440/webmetaphors.html.

Tokar, Alexander 2007. Internet Metaphors: A Cross-Linguistic Perspective. *Culture, Language & Representation* 5, 209-220.

Traugott, Elisabeth Closs and Richard B. Dasher 2002. *Regularities in Semantic Change*. Cambridge et al.: Cambridge University Press.

Ullmann, Stephen 1970. *Semantics. An Introduction to the Science of Meaning*. Reprint. Oxford: Blackwell.

Waldron, Ronald A. 1979. *Sense and Sense Development*. Second Edition. London: Deutsch.

Woiskunski, Alexander 2001. Internetmetaphern. In: Schmid, Ullrich (ed.), pp. 289-316.

WordNet. http://wordnet.princeton.edu/perl/webwn.

Wozny, Lucy Anne 1989. The Application of Metaphor, Analogy, and Conceptual Models in Computer Systems. *Interacting with Computers* 1 (3), 273-283.

Zipf, George Kinsley 1949. *Human Behavior and the Principle of the Least Effort*. New York: Hafner.

www.ingramcontent.com/pod-product-compliance
Ingram Content Group UK Ltd.
Pitfield, Milton Keynes, MK11 3LW, UK
UKHW021841210426
5322IPUK00022B/404